Only the
Dead Are
Forgiven

Poems by Greg Kuzma

The Backwaters Press

Copyright © 2015 by Greg Kuzma

Cover design by Bristol Creative, www.bristolcreative.com

Cover Art, "The Blind Leading the Blind" or "The Parable of the Blind,"
Flemish Renaissance, Pieter Bruegel the Elder, 1568, National Museum of
Capodimonte, Naples, Italy.

Book design by SR Desktop Services

Photo of poet by Alex Kuzma, copyright © 2015 Greg Kuzma

The Backwaters Press
3502 N 52nd Street
Omaha, Nebraska 68104-3506
Jim Cihlar, Editor
Greg Kosmicki, Editor Emeritus
Rich Wyatt, Associate Editor
www.thebackwaterspress.org
thebackwaterspress@gmail.com

Copyright © 2015 by Greg Kuzma
First printing, May 2015

Printed in the United States of America

ISBN 13: 978-1-935218-36-4
Library of Congress Control Number: 2015933061

Also by Greg Kuzma

Sitting Around, Lillabulero Press, 1969
Something at Last Visible, Zeitgeist, 1969
Eleven Poems by Greg Kuzma, Portfolio 2, 1971
The Bosporus, Hellric Publications, 1971
Harry's Things, Apple Press, 1971
Poems by Greg Kuzma, Three Sheets, 1971
Song for Someone Going Away, Ithaca House, 1971
Good News, Viking Press, 1973
What Friends Are For, The Best Cellar Press, 1973
A Problem of High Water, West Coast Poetry Review, 1973
The Buffalo Shoot, The Basilisk Press, 1974
The Obedience School, Three Rivers Press, 1974
A Day in the World, Abattoir Editions, 1976
Garden Report, Volunteer Maple Press, 1977
Nebraska, The Best Cellar Press, 1977
Adirondacks, Bear Claw Press, 1978
Village Journal, The Best Cellar Press, 1978
For My Brother, Abattoir Editions, 1981
A Horse of a Different Color, Illuminati, 1983
Everyday Life, Spoon River Poetry Press, 1983
Of China and of Greece, Sun, 1984
A Turning, Stormline Press, 1988
Wind Rain and Stars and the Grass Growing, Orchises, 1993
Good News, Carnegie Mellon Classic Contemporary, 1994
Grandma, The Best Cellar Press, 1995
What Poetry Is All About, Blue Scarab Press, 1998
Getting the Dead Out, Midwest Quarterly, 2001
McKeever Bridge, Sandhills Press, 2002
All That Is Not Given Is Lost, The Backwaters Press, 2007
A Day in the World, Lewis-Clark Press, 2009
For My Brother, Lewis-Clark Press, 2009
Selected Early Poems, Carnegie Mellon University Press, 2010
Mountains of the Moon, Stephen F. Austin State University Press, 2012
Robert Frost, Stephen F. Austin State University Press, 2014

ONLY THE DEAD ARE FORGIVEN

For
the amazing one,
the future now

"Only the dead are forgiven."—Phil Ochs

Small Talk

For the Mayors at The Sportsman Bar

I used to hate it. I would turn
imperious, withholding my outrage—
I could not be approached—on what
level beg you inquire?—my health?—
I was above it all, like God, in the clouds,
while far below the ants touched feelers
on their endless walks. The self, my dear,
is tiered, like a pagoda, or temple the
Aztecs built, stairs leading up, and
above those—where they stopped—
and my head turned away—maybe
my head on my fist—but a fist, mind
you, come no nearer—the thoughts
are lofty, wings sprout from the forehead,
lift off gently in the slightest breeze,
like Mercury, or some other god,
the messenger, so fleet of foot,
where thoughts as from the brow
of Zeus shivered in the air! Once in a
while I would touch down, as even
the lofty rich in their private jet—
to refuel—Learing above us
all that time—the ants below—to the fuel dump,
maybe not even
get out, but buzz a little talk to
the tower, then they are off again, the
necessary rudiments notwithstanding,
a quick and decorous motion—and if
in public, moving the hand as if to
dismiss—as if to push away beyond
consideration. There was nothing

to say. No one to speak with—who
knew my private language of regard?
And then I was off!—called away—
compelled by some desire or
urgent phone call from the soul. Or
it was some long-defended portion
of the mind, embattled, entrenched,
overly built up as in earthworks
after years of assault and battery,
a fort besieged for years grows
layers of protection, endless, to
foil attackers. I thought, if asked,
I had a case. Put in adage form it
might go "Waste not the coin
of the realm, the precious breath
of the soul's beleaguered lungs,
tongue's eloquence—on trifles."
Who dreamt of speeches made as
before God—who else was worthy?—
turning at last to note the waitress
at my coffee cup, a moth around
the bulb—as I had seen my friend Hugh
do it—who was "tough on the working
class"—look down over thin razors
of glasses, then in a gesture all but
imperceptible, like listening with your
ear nuzzling some telescope stretched
a hundred miles across an empty desert—
to pick up some residual trace—The Big Bang's
after-image of its aftershock, a hundred-
zillionth echo slung along the wide spine
of The Milky Way—or is it God's breath?—
left over from when into Adam he
poured, inflating those thin bags
in which we carry all our wealth of life—
and Hugh would flick his wrist,

which then became, in later transfor-
mations, a wag of his finger, just
the last joint a-twitch, to signal
his displeasure. It used to irk me
watching him—proving we are known but
by degrees, the bachelor and the master
and the PhD, notwithstanding,
but by subtle shades of arrogance and
"guilt"—I would like to say. Each
of us blind to his own offense, only
in the shallow river of the other
where that thin veneer of self gives
back a little ghostly image of the onlooker.
I would watch him, not even knowing
I did: and he taught me much.
Perhaps my compassion was awakened
in his abuse? Some slight moment of
gratuitous disdain, the other standing
there, more like a shadow or a post,
who had waited on us for an hour.
How I had seen myself in her or him,
at first to be more so in the cell of
myself, ourselves, and then to watch
a man I called my friend betray some
thing I did not know I loved. I speak
with each person now. Years later
still rushing outwards from that place
where I knelt down and kissed the earth,
weeping for my offense. I cannot get
enough of the streets now. Having
thrown off my last raiment, the self-
regarding drapery of my form—these
are the scabs on my knees where I knelt
in the dirt, like yours. Anything might
be my starting place. Who sits by my
door in his demeanor, writing to read,

reading, then they will fall to the seat
beside me. Energy passes as between
the bumbled flower and the bee,
each other to the other drawn, or
lover to lover—so many now I love—
to speak in rapt amazement, in the
common miracle of voice, hearing each
word in common currency, a courtesy
as if the first word spoken or heard.
Around me as I work the babble of
voices blending symphonic, while
now and then one argument snakes out
as if presented by the oboe, charming
the snake, or like smoke rising, hypnotic
in its spiral, spinning the whole full mind.
I used to wonder how a one could be
or find himself to be but a bassoon, a
buffalo, or, as Hayden says, "the walloping
trombone," and carry but the range of
walloping, or as in the case of the bassoon—
dirigible dirge on a foggy night, yet this
is too the voice of beauty, and well within
my range. Nasal, as if with pinched nostrils,
or throaty, or as if through gapped teeth,
sucking on a straw, as one might be
being of a nervous temperament, meanwhile
mixed with sidelong glances, or may drop
his head to study perhaps his watch.
Armand is a wonder! Yesterday he came
in hesitant, standing long at the door,
hugging his handmade cane out of some
twisted overgrown twig, knotted and
hand-rubbed. Wearing a huge camouflage
bib—itself which seemed to speak.
Foliage luxurious folded upon itself
endlessly, as all around us voices

swirled like vines twisting into flowers
and the nubs of words. It is all
camouflage, from the garden grown
into the jungle of the now. No color
to stand out beyond the rest, no speech
to resonate within the wood, but in
a true democracy of souls. We are all
on one level now—breathing in and out
the language of each other—to dance
in each other's words, first you leading
me up some Rushmore of your mother's face,
I put my hand out into but one pore
beside her nose, my story weather,
a brim of sunlight flaring in her eyes.
It is all a fast-change marvel this interchange
of syllables, first I changing the flat on
your car, to squat beside you in the dirt,
singing you my poem as I spin the lug nuts,
wearing each other's shirts against the cold.
Four men I know sit here behind me
now, an ex-mayor, retaining his
decisiveness, the manager of water and
light, and then another mayor, whose
house is just north down my street, and
Loren, of bowed legs, who sings so
sweetly in the band George formed.
Among them, by common decree,
dances the bird of mutual regard. It
floats, or seems to, just beyond their
reach, coaxed upwards on the heat of
their ideas—Is it merely their breath that
keeps it up? Poised on the updraft of
their common love. Their spirits lift
it high, to rise toward some tomorrow,
sustained in the head-height of their
laughter. It is the bird of peace of mind,

aglow in the faint bloom of the cheeks
of their good company, flushed in their
excitement of giving. Each in turn
adjusts the altitude, or ruffles its feathers
just a bit to drop down in new urgency.
Sweet nothings they whisper to it,
for who can tell what will sustain it
next? What spangle of water, what seed
of thought nourish it? And nothing
ever comes of what they do. Their
happy harmony dissolves, their booth
a bench of stone on the world's windy
hill. Then may I turn to see the table
empty, or one lone speaker, silent,
his hands snared still in invisible threads
and silks of dying speech. Then they
are here once more. And now a rush
behind me, a bush of tangled syllables
erupts into flame, then a roiling to a
boil, the pot's hot splashing, cackles in
the hen yard through which the fox of
mischief wends his way, gobbling and
gagging in white feathers, surprised it
is really themselves they are of,
propelled as by some inner witness.
We are of each other. No stranger who
is not my brother. No woman who is
not my mother, daughter who is not
my son. Language is our current and
our currency, by blood joined at the
tongue, our words on wings dance and
hover in the human heat of thought. To
be is to speak. Breathless in this goodly
company, father, brother, sister, mother,
so we whisper small talk to each other.

The Marsh

For Craig Nolting

Craig mentions "The Marsh,"
how the river comes down around
the point of Sandhills bluff
to fill the marsh or make its
winds and bends, and I see something
out of Sherlock Holmes, "The Hound
of the Baskervilles," walking around
in a swamp at midnight, seeing a
ghostly light, or being chased
through the bog under a pale moon.
In the Adirondacks we would fish
Death Brook, a little brown-gold
stream, reddish brown my father
said, from tannic acid of the trees
which fell into the water and rotted,
and gold from the bottom sand,
upstream from where it crossed
the road, up the old dump road
where as kids we went to watch
the bears eat garbage. We did it
three or four times. The Brook
came through a meadow, hidden by
the banks of high grass, and
you were always stepping down
into glue, putting your foot in,
then regretting it, and trying
to pull it out again. You'd pull
and the boot would stay in the muck,
your foot slide out, and there was
always that thought in the back
of your mind, no, in the front

of your mind as you walked there,
that some time soon you'd step
into a hole and not get out,
just leave your hat floating
on the surface shiny black from
oil and swamp gas. The Brook
was there. It came around a bend,
then made another bend. There was
no straightaway, just the endless
turnings of the Brook. We caught
trout there, attracted by the cold
spring water. They lived in the
pools, crowded out, and never got
large, never large enough to eat
each other, just a lot of little
fish. You'd throw your worm in
and the free-for-all would begin,
and soon you'd have a Brookie in
the grass at your feet. They were
good eating. Then you'd have to
take another step, get off to find
another spot, and all the same
fear would come back. The fear
gave an edge to the mind, it
sharpened it, and I remember how
my heart would pound the whole
time, going in, fishing, and coming
out again, pulling the long boot up
out of the slime, and stand there on
the road, covered with it. Maybe
it happened only once like that,
to keep me all these years, to keep
in my mind some special place,
and amplify its image when the
word was "marsh" up on The Snake,
north of Hyannis, thirteen-hundred

miles away. I put my fears to rest
and followed Craig, and Jeremy,
who came along in his San Francisco
Forty-Niners jacket, shiny gold,
like silk, as the faint rain fell.
It was after a sunny afternoon,
and this to be the evening fishing,
going upstream into The Marsh.
We went on up into The Marsh.
It was lovely there. There were
no monsters crawling in the bog.
I took a step or two, along my side,
and my feet held. I took another
step. At my feet the sand banks
leveled out, the high ridges of sand
had all washed down along the sides
of the stream. Grasses grew there
in abundance. I looked and looked
and tried to see them all, but
everywhere I looked some other shape
took my eye. Proceeding west, we
entered a dream world. Each bend
of the stream produced new wonders.
Strange plants grew on fingers of
land where the stream curved back
against itself in its coming.
They were not tall, but adjusted
to my height, as if someone who
knew me had gone on ahead and
cut the tall ones down, or took them
off with a whisper of breeze. I
had feared I would not be able to
see where my foot went, but it
was no problem, I just brushed
through. My legs, wet from the
stream, brushed against the grass

and I went forward, edging along
the stream. My heart stopped
pounding. Here and there some
water had escaped the bed of the
stream and spread out thin over
the sand. Hummocks of grass grew
in the water, placed there for my
walking. The rain stopped, the
sun came out. Blocked by the bluff
to my right, still it shown off
left, disclosing trees that came down
to the stream side. I walked toward
it, casting my lure. Though there was
sun ahead, bathing the trees and where
the stream bent down towards us, the
water here grew darker, deeper, more
mysterious. Runs that might have looked
shallow or gold now took on a dark
amber color. Minutes passed. Then
the pools darkened further. Always
the current came on, but slower, yet
perceptible. The breeze died, there
was no sound except for whatever noise
I made, going. And then I heard the
water sounds. No gurgling of deep
dead things, bubbling up from unseen
depths, but a clean sound, like a
hose running in a garden. The water
was clear and pure, cold against
my feet. There was still light
to see, but not enough to glare
the water. I could see in, into
the dark, but still notice the
surface swirling. The water was
alive. It came around a bend ahead
and pushed against the grass along

the edge. It swirled against the
bank and formed a tiny whirlpool
which came on toward me and swirled
past. Then another formed where
the water curled and rolled and
came on. I was hearing the sound
of its turning. Then where I
stood, where the stream turned
again, a little, and the water
looked deep, some of it lifted
itself and mushroomed up,
erupting gently toward the surface
like some spring erupting from the
depths. It seemed to hold in place,
amidst the general swirling as
the stream came on. I stood there.
Off to my left the red-winged
blackbirds sang. I can't describe
their sounds. Not cries of alarm,
not even calls to each other, just
a happy tune at evening, letting
the day go. I let the day go.
I had no fear. Whatever I had
taken there, some burden I carried,
fell from me. All the failures
of my life, all my little angers
and complaints, slipped from me.
Were they carried away in the water?
I do not know. But they were gone.
I felt entirely free. My senses
opened. I smelled the air, full of
the chill of the stream and the evening.
I forgot my fishing, whatever ambition
I had had. I wanted only to stand
where I was, unmoving, and stay like
that. A minute passed. I heard

only the water, the gentle passing
of the water as it came and went.
I stood there, feeling the wet of
my shoes, the damp of my pants from
the stream. And then I did not feel
even that. I stood there for a year.
A decade passed, and I did not
notice. A century turned, and I
knew I was seeing the place as it
was and would be. I knew I was
seeing back in time, a thousand
years, long before my struggles or
the struggles of my family. This
was a place unchanged by anyone.
Men had plotted murder in the dark
and gone out in the sun and done
their deeds. Bombs fell,
cities burned. The race collected
its dead and buried them. Collected
its thoughts, and its regrets, and
saw what it had learned, and went on
ahead, and made the same mistakes
again. The stream came on. The
water made the turn ahead where I
looked and came past. New water,
continuous, without interruption,
rounded the bend and came on
towards me. It filled my eyes.
The waters of my eyes cleared
in the oncoming waters. The waters
of my blood moved with the movement
of the stream, and I was at peace.
I looked around. Craig was ahead
of me, standing in his waders.
It was almost dark. At my feet
where I turned to look, new ferns

were rising up out of the grasses.
They were only a few inches tall,
only a portion of their total height.
They were fresh and green, a tender
lighter green, just beginning to
unfurl. I bent my arm and touched
the tip of one. And then we turned
around and walked back to our camp.

Gord's Gold, Volume II

I am loyal to the month
I wrote the poem about the dog,
when the snows swirled, and then
bought the tape of the folksinger,
which I hated, but kept forcing back
into the player, driving to work,
and told a student friend about it,
how I was going to write a letter
to the singer to complain. We are
a fast society and throw away what
won't work, and buy things just to
buy things so if the songs are shit,
no one will remember very long but
get on with our lives. Sitting
where he is, in comfort, plucking
out a tune, a hundred thousand shoppers
making their mistake, writing it off,
and he won't have to work another year.
But the tape changed. It worked on
the nerves of my ear. It whispered
down some corridor, where at the
other end a window opened, curtains
blew, and love had failed, or someone
had grown old. I said to myself,
Gordon Lightfoot wears the common
doom, and wears it lightly, here is
how he goes on writing past the time
of greatest inspiration. We do not
surrender. Some kill themselves,
but most of us go on, struggling,
trying to make sense of our lives.
New beauty comes to us, hanging its
head down, dragging its feet a bit.

I heard his middle-age singing,
singing to mine. And I forgave.
Oh, not all the songs are good.
Some never fully emerge out of the
tangle of their melodies, or if there
is a sweetness in the tune, the words
are wrong. I lamented the absence of
one great song, "Talking in Your Sleep,"
and may still write to him about it.
What are listeners for but to confirm
our taste, or not confirm it. There's
one incredible romp of a piece, "Alberta
Bound," which surges and comes rushing
out at you, you want to go skipping along,
off to old Alberta. It reminds me a little
of "Alabama Bound," the great Leadbelly song.
Another one is haunting. The refrain is
"Bless you all and keep you," and he
sings it often, almost too often, but
it's so gorgeous you want to cry.
I wanted to, finally, after I figured
it all out. This one makes me think
how anyone would want to say these
words, to reach that special moment
in your life when you are done taking,
when you don't need another thing
but can look out at every person and
wish them well. I have felt that.
To take me in a moment and shake me
up and down, then let me drop. I'll
get all worked up, and call somebody
on the phone, but then get shy. You
want to sing like Gordon Lightfoot does,
to sweep your voice in blessing through
the hall, then later, after the concert,
go down to stand by the door,

and take them every one by hand as
they leave, or in your arms. Such things
do not always come. I've been working
on myself, and then, in my spare time,
I work on my father. Five letters have
I sent him over the winter and spring,
five at least, and a couple long ones,
choked with news. To give him all
the glory I can give, and the heartaches,
he who lives a thousand miles away,
I never see but once a year. I'm
trying to wear him down. And finally
I did. My most recent letter I started
to close with, "Well, write," but then
caught myself and said, "Oh I know you
won't, you never do, but oh hell, let
me say it anyway." That smoked him
out. A hundred combinations of entreaties
and apologies and tempting bits of news,
to try to bring him forth among the
living still, to dance with me and
Gordon in a ring. It worked. On
Mother's Day he called, and talked
to Jax, thinking it was Barb, and
wished her a good day. What a shock.
We go on stronger after that, renewed
in the faith. We trust a little deeper
in things, let go more gently when we
go, forgive the stranger quicker, grant
to anyone the effort of their lives.
Bless you, father, keep you, I'll
hear Gordon sing. And crank the music
up when that song comes on. Oh to have
written that! And thought of the poets
toiling in the silence of their rooms,
toiling in the chaos of our minds,

without the sweet, unrolling ribbon of
a melody, to lead us on, to lead us
down beside the healing waters.
We are not complete. We yearn
for what we lack. The son not the
father, not knowing his life, or
what he feels. I go around without
that, longing for it, and the aching
of its absence makes me kind. Without
guitar I read some poems I wrote for
Jeff, when we had his friends to the
house. My voice went naked in the
air, finding its own pitch and movement.
We cannot have everything. I had
their love. I had my life to live.
Then in March I bought *Gord's Gold,
Volume II.* Now I have my father's
phone call, out of the blue, who
calls once in ten years, the wire
should have melted with the heat of
that miracle. There are other songs
on the tape. I can't think of the
titles now. They're mostly on the
second side. Lightfoot has a pale,
thin voice. Sometimes it seems to have
no resonance at all, no depth,
but like some disembodied thing, a
butterfly perhaps, if it could sing,
would sound like him.

The Parable of the Sticks

For Jack Hill

And so the man in the house
looked out upon what passed for him a yard
to survey and approve these reaches
whereupon to his dismay numerous
large sticks appeared, appearing to have
fallen from out of consoling limbs
to make a scatter over the face of
things, whereupon he rose, getting up
actually from out of his easy chair,
when he had been waiting to collapse
into for—what was it?—years?—to earn
that blessed respite in the wars of time—
and went out, gathering them up,
first in one arm, making a big load,
then across his body, and would drop one
hand down almost kneeling, to pick
another stick until, all the large
sticks were gathered in, and stuffed
them away, for later or for burning,
and went back into the house again. He
sat. He attended to his paper. He
was almost settled in, that sleep that
comes to he who waits, but being maybe
greedy to know the good that he had
done, looked out over the yard, expecting
to see a width of green, from tree to
shining tree, uninterrupted, some splendid
(perhaps?) equilibrium? But what was this?
Each place he looked he saw a stick,
not large, but a stick plain enough,
and would remark how could he not

have seen them once upon a time,
being so diligent and all, only to see
how they were of a smaller size, and so
on, and yet the very essence of the
thing itself. He was amused, yet weary
too, for how much of this thing he might
have read, and known it just as well, or
having had it told to him would have sufficed—
why was it he must learn each thing in
turn, himself, by the sheer doing? And
so he got up once more, put on the stick-
fetching coat, the heavy boots that cry out
"This is now." And he was gone. And they
were everywhere. No place he looked he
did not see one—sticks of a color, sticks
inches long, so that they were hard to
carry, and had to be grasped in one hand,
until he could not hold them all. He got
the wheelbarrow out. He called the cats
to him. He sat down and petted the cats.
Were they part of it all? And the
sun dispersing all across the lawn. A
few leaves down. Until he was done. He
turned his back, he would not go in,
then turned back quickly to the perfect
lawn. In seconds it had been overrun. In
seconds thousands of smaller sticks, yet
sticks quite visible, stared back at him.
It seems in fact that what was once
the lawn now boasted a forest of sticks.
There were too many—were there not?—
and he but one person, and a wonderful
unease came over him. So was his life like
this, in all respects? How that very week
he did the meeting, how it had loomed large
in his mind for days, only to be met quite well,

decidedly, and with success. Great warmth
passed among those gathered, where before
he had seen no harmony, or had imagined
the worst, and yet...and yet. And left
the meeting and walked down the hall, his
feet almost rising from the floor and almost
flying out a bit, or kicking up his heels,
but did not, shuffling along at best, only
to find some moments later what seemed
like an annoyance threatened to erupt,
a small conference over a poem—was it
evidentiary? Did it signify some earlier
failure? The deafness of the father?
The fatal or near fatal flaw? Some
parallel flaw? He looked at the student—
he tried to appease him—he saw that
his student was not to leave—and would
stay forever now, camped out in the office,
till right words were spoken. A turn to a
tone in the pit of a word, a quirk in the
voice, a lift, a drift, another sip of
coffee, then they were over the treacherous
spots. The cheery goodbye. The corridor
empty once more. Only to let it all wash
over him, tremendous relief, tremendous
ease, and fall down at the desk exhausted,
having come through, had he not?—having
worked it out, having earned the chair. But
what was this? This piece of an end of
paper poking out amidst the vast minutia
of his desk, this heel of the toe of the
worm, turning a little in soft light,
until the whole vast enterprise was lost—
vast rotted melon of his desk and dream—
a missed appointment, a scrawled note,
apologizing yet entreating too—a little

disappointed maybe—a name he had not seen
before amidst the frenzied roll call of
the afternoon—how had it escaped him?—
some turned tone to the way the name was
scrawled—how had he failed this one?—
what was his crime? Now it loomed large
above him like Hiroshima, or wreck beside
the road that he had made himself, whereas
no tally of great victory could speak for
an opportunity that slid, or slipped, but
notched in the run of belt loops—Is it over
the side of a well?—A rope pulled up an inch
or so, then let fall back to the dark once
more. So great failure grew up out of a
bit of ink, haphazard in an alphabet of loss,
and would it be too much to bear this time,
the hand shaking, sweat to form across the
upper lip, as he puts on his coat to now go out,
and lace the heavy burden of the boots.
It is later now. The sun, always precarious,
has fallen on its face along the hills,
and will not rise again. And he has missed its
orange skirts, which used so much to cheer him
in the old days. Now in the failed light
he works, kneels on the grass, and picks
them up—must pry them almost from the blades
of grass, then cup them in his open hands.
And this but one small portion of his vast
estates.

Chafing at the Bit

It had to be soon! Now! It had to be
yesterday, if not before! It had to be
before the paint could dry, the soup
get cold in the bowl. From insight to
inspiration to event, all in six seconds,
lickety-split. I was not one to weigh
and consider. But plunge headlong into
whatever was there. I would be like the
man who jumped into the swimming pool
before it had filled up, hitting his head,
would pass myself on a double line
going up a hill, against the flow of
traffic, in winter, miles from home,
the gas gauge empty, the motor on fire,
smoke billowing out. Or set out, midnight,
into the dark, my feet in bedroom slippers,
no time to change, no time to say goodbye.
Destination? Somewhere else! Arrival time?
Immediate. Like being zapped up in a space
ship, or sent across a room at the speed of light,
materializing on the other end almost before
the afterimage faded. I could not wait.
"Father, I cannot wait," I'd tell him,
standing there, my hands in the air, my
fingers jumping and dancing at the ends of
my arms. And could not even speak, the time
it took to get the words out might the impulse
kill, could not even tell him what it was
I wanted, the words to jam in my throat
like logs in a raging river, or one of those
wondrous jams on California roads, backed up
four or five miles, 2,000 cars involved. Would
run out of breath from my excitement, when,

coming at last into his presence, would not
have a single breath to speak—then might my
voice come softly from a world away—"Are
we going yet?"—whispered with my last ounce
of strength. It had to be immediate or I could
not believe, could not accept it as reality.
Or then some corollary of the law, written in
tears in every book of pain, how the more
I waited the worse it was, the greater was my
disappointment. Where are they now?—the wise
ones in their holy places, having traversed this
wilderness of ours, to set up shop below the
thoroughfare, to take in the worn shoes of
experience? Shoemakers to the world, and we
the fleet foot ones to seek them out. What can
the sages tell us of the heart's mad pulse
of beating onward endless unto death?
I had my father only, wise enough, at thirty,
at thirty already old—who'd put a damper on his
heart, to slow it down, or keep its mad beat
from his ears. Would be the very glacier of
our house, whatever season, nor skid on his
own melting, freezing the earth below him
all around as he moved an inch. And freeze
me too, his naked fledgling, twitching in
anticipation right at the brim of the nest.
It was always summer where I looked, always
a fresh breeze blowing in with frankincense
from Asia Minor, whispers of forgotten gold,
treasures where the rainbows rolled up high
like backs of sounding whales, spouting white
against the blue cold slate of the sea.
The dandelion was ready to explode, just
as my back was turned, its yellow face gone
white in the sun's quick wink, leaves thrust
out through their clench of buds ere the

last dim snowflake fluttered like a moth
and landed on my hand, to pulse there like
a quaking heart. Or melt to tears like me,
taking the long walk home. Each day
the world died more, slipped from my grasp,
the dawn and then, turning to run, my shoelace
catching on the gate, the shoe come loose,
I dipped to tie it back in place and it was noon,
the day already gone, light stale as bread
crumbling across the lawn, the mailman fled,
the milkman safely home in bed, and then
the evening streetlights coming on. How
could you stop time, friend? Watched how
the river ran, from left to right, from right
to left away, and went to stand in it and try
to hold it back, dip down both hands and
feel the current's driven strength. I'd try to
make my way across, perhaps to reach the other
bank, just for the sake of it, tiring of the side
I stood on, hours in its bleary study hall, wading out
boldly, then too deep for me, and the cold out
of the earth come, cutting then a wading stick,
which I might place the tip of down, to wedge
between the kiss between two rocks, then
struggle there, locked, my feet slid up upon a
slab of slippery slate, losing their grip,
and it already nine o'clock. If you looked twice
you could see the sun move, the baby bird
beside the garbage can, its tiny twitter, turning
just away, a flutter in the tree above, the mother
come to oversee, then dead when I looked back.
My pants too short, my ankles sticking out
like bolts, wrists dangling participial, down
from the sleeves of faded shirts. I sneezed once,
turning around I was old, leaves already autumn
in the yard. I'd go to get the mower out, or pick

the tiger lilies all along the sun porch side,
the door jam on a foot of fresh December snow.
Then slam the screen door running out to play,
climb up into the lap of the box elder tree,
gone these forty years so soon. Running, I ran
to school, to try to beat the clock, but fell—
to watch it run so gaily on ahead, its joyous
laughter shredded into car horns. No more
it spoke my name. Or took the long way home,
trying to outwit the savages along the hedges
waiting with their scalping knives, the cavalry
asleep around their fires miles away. My heart
raced up down stairs, on each level a thing begun
but running out of gas, the kettle steaming up
the windows all along our view of Linden
Street, water running in the tub but I already
scrubbed by wind or roughhoused by unruly
boys, racing down to turn the motor off,
to fetch the missing fountain pen, ink caked
dry from all the poems I had not found the
time to write. Night bunched its hands in
front of my eyes, inside was morning like a
coin's bright face, the sun in the palm of the
stranger's hand or hidden beneath the blur
of thimbles, lost in the trick. My father must
have felt me like the thaw that to the glacier
means the end of its composure, or like the
fire in the wood, to hasten it away, his furniture
to kindling made, there in the shack of the last
stand, stacks of rags in the garage erupting into
flames, their desires run away with them, years
of cabin fever hot in their combustion. Against
me he stood. Desert over which my flood of
river ran, to sop me up, blotter to the spilled ink
of my words, bandage to my gushing blood,
life pouring forth from the wound of life,

words pouring forth from the wounds of words.
I was a river in the desert of his timelessness,
fresh in my gush over sparkling sands,
caressing them and spreading out, picking
the gravel up, gouging a further trench, then
bunched against some rock he'd left there—
was it accident?—dispersing as I went,
spreading myself thin, as he was wont to say,
to where evaporation's afterthought peeled
my skin and there was just the amber sand again.
He counted on me to wear or run out, a spring
freshet so full of itself, by late July was gone,
all the zip of the water zapped, the rocks instead
of lifting up in proper boulder roll, in shivers
of light, stood out like ruined cathedrals
from the firestorm of German cities my eyes
first woke to. His was the sad Sargasso of
the soul. A hill to my coasting, fresh from my
descent into his neighborhood, steering madly
as I came, my soapbox racer thrown together
out of crates and sticks, stalling out against the
slope of his indifference. The phone poles,
having once leaped free, returned to their ropes
and chains. There was less air. The wind was tamed.
No matter. I had seen the clouds pass like
eyelids over the sun's deep thought. I was
no superstitious painted creature brought to
his knees by some impermanent eclipse. But
took another wild idea, unhinged from the
flange in the Monarch's spread-wide wings,
or from my sneakers with fresh dirt on them set
on the edge of the porch, covered in the soil
I remembered I had been rooted in, or I a slender
newt over the shade's wet stones, then rush
to beg him, "Might we go?" I pointed to the
round world's shoulder off to the left-behind trees.

Right to the chill cliffs of the glacier go and stand,
and crane my neck up its vast look, its long
inertia shadowed down upon me, where I stood,
knee deep in that chill dark, that winter resignation.
And so it began, our strange and tragic dance,
I as if standing on his feet, the way the child will,
waiting to be moved, at his discretion, and stand
with my arms around the backs of his knees.
All day the music played, I heard it. But still
no impetus or progress to our dance, nor had he
ever asked this dance of me, until I looked to
see if he were there at all, and not some cardboard
statue in his place. And when the music stopped,
I saw we had not moved in time with it, but
stood atop each other, as if locked, my small
weight just enough to keep his feet from motion,
and his pulse so faint, I could not hear it
from the din of mine. Often we went like this,
weekend after weekend, his life one long
postponement of my fevered schedule, till I
turned away. He would invoke against me,
as a joke, his favorite horses, the figure of the
horse wearing the bit, and maybe not too good a fit,
all its miles unrun, the spring I might have had
in my young legs reined down into our steadfast
stoop. It was all he could do to stop me in
my tracks, to tug the bit down hard, to break
my stride, to spread my river thin in the drought
of reconsidered afterthought. Once before
my father died I wish I'd asked him why it
was he would not ride the horse I was—
away—just anywhere at all—through time
and tide.

Blackbirds over Tanglewood

Bickering, they come over the
top of the dam. (Fighting with
myself, I try to write the poem
about the blackbirds.) It's
autumn, dry September. Red light
off my parked truck sharpens my
eye to see them in their myriad
crossings. (Is this the whole
bunch, I wonder, but no, there
are always more.) "Emissaries
of distance, they come calling
the far and near together when
they sing." "Keepers of the sun,"
I would like to say, "who store
in their dark cloaks the heat
of a hundred suns, the chill of
a thousand nights." Three or
four days in a row I watch them—
though I had other interests—
first with irritation, then
with amusement, then wrote about
them in another poem, where,
almost, though they appeared
occasionally, they nearly took
the poem over. Two nights
into my four I found myself
looking for them, and once,
getting there a little early,
before they make their nightly
appearance, the place was weirdly
dead. No voice rang over the
ruined lakebed of tall, desiccated
plants. And the sky empty.

And I was afraid I had seen
the end of the world. Or the
feeling I felt was of my own
death. But then they were there,
a drift of dots along a far brown
hill. Then, nearing, I could see
the motion of each one, straining
to keep its place in the body,
the living body of the flock.
Then more close still, soon they
came over me, until I saw better
a few of them, and picked them
out, and followed each one with my
eyes. Each seemed at its own
devices, "The job being to keep
aloft," and seemed to be working
hard at it, for none were graceful.
Each seemed to have a hard
time flying, yet, when they
passed, the look of the flock
was of symmetry and design, as if
"The whole partook of more than
the sum of its parts, possessed
of some higher order." Or was it
merely a trick of the eye? And
I thought of my own awkward
movements, all the years of my
growing up, my blushes, my hands
crammed in my pockets, my elbows
so jammed against my sides no one
could pry them loose, yet the
river of life flowed through me,
my daughter sat with me in my
office today, the phone rang and
I answered it, there were some
questions and I knew the answers—

"How far had I flown on unsteady
wings!" What was their sound like,
I asked myself the second or third
night out there. And imagined a
poem, not this poem, where everything
would be accounted for, the "Speed
of their color, the shape of their
gathering, the flux and flex of
their rhythm," and the sound of
their thousand wings beating and
blurring and overlapping, and all
done with great compression,
like that of a sonnet, metered by the
stroke and dip and glide, the
glide being very prominent,
in which the bird drops noticeably,
until, after it almost drops
too far, it remembers its method,
and beats its wings again. I
thought about that sound for a
week at least, then decided they
sound like "an immense sewing
machine," or like 500 little ones,
each clean and dry, or geared in
thin, delicate machine oil, so that
you almost hear the clicking of
their million parts, just barely broken
in, a sound you could learn to
work by, like "the sound of a
fan on a hot day, blowing softly
in another room." Then they go
off, "stitching the sky, drawing a
hem along a bank of clouds," which
look a lot like pillows on a
couch, "drawing a seam in the air."
I wrote this in my poem, one of

my variations on a famous
Stevens poem, which I thought
I could use, but which got too
much in my way—I had to give it
up—how I had hoped to introduce
a metaphor and let it go, let
it fly free for a while, trusting
it the way I learned to trust
the blackbirds. "Bickering,
they come across the top of the
dam," I write in a poem, calling
all the while, "articulate, but
in some forgotten tongue."
Phrases I wanted to say, phrases
they recognize some meaning in,
or how they encourage each other,
holding their flight together.
I would not be surprised to hear,
for instance, that they are weak-
sighted, and keep together for
protection, perhaps the keenest-
sighted leading the way, connected
each to each by song. Song? I
say! It is not song. More like
a cackle, or "gossip among harpies,"
almost a rudeness, they speak
of an unrelieved landscape of
dry, hard husks of encrusted seeds,
while drought has parched even
the leaves. Yellow already, from
months without rain, with the freeze
last week they seem scarcely to
have turned at all. And the lake—
Tanglewood names a lake—or used
to—the lake is a puddle now,
but their haven. I like to park

myself along one of their flight
lines, squat down amongst some
goldenrod, and watch them come
up out of the south for water,
then, cresting the top of the dam,
on some invisible mountain of air,
descend along the other side
to swirl in around the lake.
They come down "like soot,"
falling out of the air at the
last, settling along the lake
shore a "black width on brown
dirt," while others—are they
lookouts?—are they separatists?—
plop down on tall sticks of weeds,
there to totter back and forth
like souls in crisis. ("Or
like me in the morning, trying
to get my stuff together to leave
the house, shifting from foot
to foot, thought to thought,
checking for car keys, yes or no,
wallet and checkbook, pens? Are
they in my case? And so on...")
Shouting all the while in their
great obscurity. Then, having
slaked their thirst (it's hard to
see what they do, but I imagine
them leaning down, each one to
wedge up a beak of water, doing
it all without arms, as if their
arms are tied behind their backs,
some athletic maneuver we are
always being asked to perform at
parties, where everybody's drunk).
Then they are airborne again.

They rise in a sudden rush, almost
a "whoosh," a large exhalation,
and then they fly off somewhere
else. Within minutes they are
back—"Or are these other birds"?—
and I was never sure how many
separate flocks make their home
there. Three groups I saw in
the air at one time, in one perhaps
two hundred birds, but before I
could try to count, another
flock blew past. One night they
came on for a good ten minutes,
remnants of larger groups, even
a straggler or two—had he been
asleep, or lost?—making his
desperate uphill climb—they
always look like that, like they're
going uphill, the whole sky an
invisible mountain range—but I
could not be sure if birds I had
seen a minute before at the lake
were not coming around again,
as in some vast playground game,
"or circulation of the blood"—
in any case it was an endless
stream. A week later I was back
again. We had had our freeze.
The trees at the west end of
the dam were gold now, gold
enough, so that the birds flying
there, between me and the trees,
looked like a dark inlay, carved
letters or figures below while
sumac poured out its heart. I
wanted my camera then, or a

long memory, or better words.
(I wanted to say the pretty part
about the sumac.) Perhaps to
capture the whole unruly mob in
a haiku, ignoring the breadth
of their frenzy, capturing only
contrasted colors, or their
elevation over gold leaves.
That night they did their same
routine, of not being able to
decide where they wanted to be,
preferring at first, it seemed,
the south, where they disappeared
into that remoteness, only to come
back again or be replaced by
another flock. And always
the same great to-do, never
losing heart, never tiring,
but coming on with the same
absorbed enthusiasm, to swarm
in over the lake again. I
would like a mind like that,
a thousand separate energies
all blended, or, in a moment,
to rise at once, turning all
one-sided to the world, to
have thought speak with one
voice, in concert, and—
seeing the world again appear
as it has, the same faces,
the same problems, resume,
perhaps, offering the same
solution, but without exhaustion,
without discouragement, without
tedium. But I have not achieved it,
something of their wisdom,

just watching them, seeing
how inexhaustible they are,
and each time doing the same
things, but not exactly in
the same sequence, I took all
this as a model for my own life,
vowing against all awful drudgery,
that I would not complain again
at the way another year comes
round, having to do my leaves
again, under the trees, for
what?—the hundredth time!—
this time I will do them with
joy, I swear it, and lots of
jabber with my neighbors over
the sideyard fence, as I am
instructed by the blackbirds.
All that shouting—is it hello
or farewell?—"And will they
persist through any weather,
until the back of winter is broken"?
In the ideal poem about the
blackbirds, I can get one of my
favorite lines in, how the wind
becomes a "wind of wings," or
call them "a river of gossip,"
as I do in another poem. Let's
bring the best saying together
with the best seeing, I say,
and speak altogether our praise
of weather, sun or heartbeat,
as they do, as they are not
suppressed but call wholeheartedly
from their stand of trees, where
one large flock has come down,
darkening the leaves, a little

night working its way around
the lake rim with news or
warning—"Beware, they say,
from sharp beaks, or are they
laughing"? Now, tonight, a
full moon rises in the east,
shimmers a little on the horizon,
shaking its broad full face,
then pales to climb up toward
me where I sit. (The blackbirds
seem especially clamorous here
at the day's end.) (Or is it
winter they talk of?)—in the
same antic postures, dotting
the sky above me, moving in
to settle in around the lake.
Happy, tired from craning
my neck to follow them, glad
to be writing my poem to the
earth, stiff from my crouch
in the tall grasses, I say
good-bye to the birds for
another year, and all the time,
all the time working on the poem,
working on the ultimate poem
about the blackbirds. Here
is how it goes so far, the
first part goes, in its eighth
revision—"Bickering, they come,
over the top of the dam,
birds of a feather, birds of
a feather, see how they rise
and fall, see how they rise
and fall together.

Keeping Time

For Carole

I do not think that I would like to
live forever. I like my role as
fellow victim. Time that lays
her hand on me, and bids me come.
Time that sits beside me in the
car, now and then reaches out to
dial the station for the time and
weather. Let Time undo me,
I am ready. Two days ago,
I saw her handiwork. C's face.
We crossed the hall between us.
What had it been?—ten years—
from washing her face in that
River. Almost the light was gone,
the skin red and dry. Nor is there
ointment from the candle flame
to bring back youth to that face.
And did her heart leap up at
seeing me?—my own ravages?
(We hugged each other there
like savages.) We hugged
each other, whispering,
agreeing not to tell. No one
speaks Time's truth. We are
all liars when love's face
hardens or the light fades.
Around her mouth, from which
poems issue, dressed in Time's
beautiful ironies, the creases
of our argument. From long into
the night, of nights unending,
talking with Time, Time that will

make poets of us all. We crossed
the hall, there was time before
her talk in the big room.
Time to repent, time to recover
some forgotten theme. Knowing
she was coming to my school,
I dug around the office, looking
for that great sestina she had
written once. I could not find
it, then remembered I had
published it myself. Time that
is gentle with us now and then,
Time that restores us to that Time
Long Gone. There it was I found it
in an early book, held in my hand,
feeling the years melt, the book
no longer draped in dust—draped
in doubt—loved now for what it
is, for the fact of itself, like C,
like myself as well—as in Time
once we had gone blinded,
now Time in her patience
opens new our eyes. There in the
hall we hugged, Time's secret
wedged between us, seeing how
well we had kept Time together,
separated by our thousand miles,
our own unique disasters—
though pain has turned
our language private and
possessed, Time works her
translation intact between us,
Time's Esperanto tingles our tongues.
My God where had she been
all this long time? That book
she signed for me in 1985—
ten years ago—and this our

anniversary of that—in Time's
River we had swum, never to be
again in the same place, swept
along, and came out changed,
Time's fingerprints all over us,
still kicking in our thrash of feet,
buoyed in that mother gel.
It is on my tongue now, that
river, on my lips a kiss. There
we were, just out of the river,
shaking ourselves dry a moment,
just before her great day was to
start, standing in that little bit
of Time afforded. Was why
we shook our heads like that, to
shake ourselves dry of tears.
At her reading later I sat in
the back, so as to disappear
into the twists and turns of Time,
far from her standing place,
though we were twins in Time,
my hair more gray, perhaps,
just sat and let Time's words
wash over me. "Let her swim
in the current, it is her time,"
I said. Ever at our elbows she
takes down our words, ever
the poet herself within us,
stenographer of grief and joy,
ever she adjusts the pulse accorded
with our own, as what we cannot
help but find beats out its own
good time in the line. In our
poems ever the river shines,
the current moves, the journey
forges its way. And we cannot
escape except at last. Then,

silent, the tongue as quiet as a
silhouette, the tremble gone out
of the pen...in us the river
moves. Tides flow and ebb,
the moon above our shoulders
marks the time. Hearing her
words my own awoke in me,
the sunlight dazzle atop the tip
ends of her talk, and then that
wondrous undertow to lodge us
there more deeply in the sands,
the amber golden sands of Time.
Here in the room with C, wearing
the blue of oceans in her eye,
the waters of her words poured
forth a steady stream and turned
The Wheel of Time on which I
rode caught in a moment's thought.
Then the reading ended, racquetball
beckoned, the sauna was hot,
Rick made some great shots,
here and there, where the ball
hung steady in the air, almost as
if Time itself had stopped, I thought
of poets and their magic rewind,
Time on the rebound held in
enchanted space and time,
and C, off on her plane perhaps
by now, an extra hour burning
in her brain, younger for our
applause, younger in our drench
of yin and yang, writing in her shock,
perhaps in trembling hands as
pinched as mine—"How old
Greg looks!"—too many nights
out late, too many poems to write—
"Oh what the years have wrought."

For the Want of the Nail

"The shoe was lost." My father said.
For the want of the shoe, the horse
was lost. And I saw the horse, I think,
out wandering around, far from the road,
eating berries maybe, or soaking his sore
hoof in a pond. For the want of the horse
the rider was lost. And I experienced a
climbing progression, seemingly upwards
in consequence, upwards in the natural order,
though perhaps I preferred horses to
people, not knowing horses but afraid
of people. Horses were on all the
shows, *The Lone Ranger*, with Silver,
so steadfast and reliable, and Scout,
Tonto's pinto, and then the horses of
The Cisco Kid and Pancho—(how alike
in name these two sidekicks, Pancho
and Tonto, almost the same sounds).
Horse and rider, one package, a blur
amidst the cactus and the sage. I
had seen on TV, newly made, such
exploits as the famous cinematic leap
onto the back of the horse of the bad-
guy rider—shooting all the while, till
he was out of bullets, then throwing
his six-gun back as a last resort,
half-heartedly, to wing past the head
of our hero. And then the leap,
onto the shoulders of the hunching man,
pulling him off in the dirt. The horses
going on, then circling back, to be
seen nibbling grass in the final frames.
Horse and rider, together as one.
The world so wide, the deserts wild

and dry. A man on foot—what could
such a one do in those days? But fall
down headlong in the dust, his big
hat rolling free, to let the killing sun
bake down on him. There was little shade.
You might lean against a tall saguaro,
follow the sun across the sky, but have
the world swim up before your eyes
in curtains of heat, waggling and swaying
till you fell, dazed, delirious. Scorpions
might build their nest beneath the rock you
lay your hand upon, the fingers clenched,
then opening, to signal the end. I did not
see the nails put into the shoe, but at the
village blacksmith, always some burly
character, bearded, with a big washboard
chest, barrel for a belly, wearing a dark apron,
there might be a scene or two where he
would take the horse's foot upon his knee,
then pound it firmly. From hard riding
the nail worked free. And then what?
Maybe another? Father never said. Maybe
all it took was one, just the first nail and
then the shoe was lost. By this he tried to
show me the value of small things. I
with my head in the clouds, dreaming of
glory, reading adventure books or Classics
Comics, I was all for the grand scenes,
the blazing swordfight on the precipice,
or jousting in the tournament, bearing down
upon each other, each with his huge long lance,
to punch a hole in one of them, like into a can
of Coke. And then the music rose. My father
was a craftsman. He didn't appear in the
movies or the books, except in the background,
lugging a cart of wood, or passing by. He

was the skittish one who did not fight,
who did not dare, but tended his flocks,
or chopped wood in the yard, sharpening
his axe. For want of the nail, he said—and
I had seen him take the hammer over one,
and pound it firm and home, or get it started
with a tap, then hit it good, taking the whole
head of the hammer back, behind his head,
and then with one blow strike home. Sometimes
he might strike it wrong, and bend it, but then
make the next blow from a different angle,
persuading the nail back on its course again,
straight to the heart. It squeaked as it went,
the wood resisting, then closing behind it
all around, its fibers holding fast. Then, when
it was almost home, giving it the one final
burnishing blow, rolling the hammer head
so as to shine the head of the nail a little,
like a little flourish, the way he'd make below
his name a long scroll, curved and rolled on
each end, then crisscrossed in the middle, to
signal that the signature was now complete.
Quiet work it was he did, like writing one's own
name, but signing like a king, to honor the common
man in his humanity. He wanted to let me know
that work counted for something, that it was not
all glory, that someone made the guns that fired
non-stop, a couple hundred rounds without
reloading, and shot all the bad guys down. He
even had guns too, was always working on them,
grinding parts—I saw where he'd made the hammer
for an old muzzle loader, then tried to blue it
down to match the color of the ancient iron,
only it looked still new. Or the reamer rod—
I don't know what to call it—that hangs beneath
the barrel of the old Colt Army, you unhinge

to push the cloth and ball into the cylinders.
He showed me how to do it. It would take
ten or fifteen minutes to load the Colt. We
had cast the bullets on the stove in the cellar,
in the little rusty iron pot, chunks of lead,
so thick and gray, so heavy in the hand,
melting down like silver butter in the pan.
I loved how the lead, so dull from oxidation,
took on a bright color when it pooled in the
pot. You had to skim the slag off—"slag"
was the word, I think—with a little skimmer—
or maybe the word was sludge—something like
that, something unwanted, where the mouth
turns grim against the teeth, the jaw set in
objection. The molds were small, some of
them, and would heat up fast, though sometimes
the first ball would not "take," would not be
"fully poured" inside. You'd open the mold
and one whole side might not be fully formed—
how sad that was—and made the breath
catch in my throat. Each mold had a cover
plate, with a hole in the center where the lead
got poured, and would fill up right to the top
of the plate. The plate had a hinge, and a big
"flange," I think he called it—that you'd strike
against a hard surface, the cement floor
or the big steel work plate on his workbench.
This would force the flange "to sheer,"
cutting off the neck of the poured lead ball.
Even so the bullet had to be sanded, the lead
"tit" he called it, filed or sanded smooth. If
we were casting "balls" I'd roll the ball around
on sandpaper, but if we were casting "wads"—
"wad cutters" he called them—you could take
the wad and slide it back and forth on the
paper, smoothing the tit. Or was the word

"nub"? It was a lot of work. Then the table
set up in the field, facing the dirt bank where
we had the cans set up. Fifteen minutes to load
the six chambers, each with its black powder,
then the percussion cap on each "nipple."
We had a special measuring device for the
powder, then a swatch of shirt to place as
the wad. It would start "snug," with then a
special tool to seat the wad in the mouth of
each cylinder, then unhinge the collapsing
ramrod down and pull it toward the handle
of the gun, thus seating the wad upon the powder.
That was the old way. That's where so many
centuries went, that was what killing took.
Sometimes in movies they show gunfighters
using the old cap-and-ball revolvers,
but never the slow work of reloading. We did
that, it was not photogenic. Father'd have
his shooting glasses on, perhaps his reading
glasses, so as to get the powder measure right,
pouring it in close up so as not to spill.
Then fumble with the bullet, seating it, time
and again, around the cylinder until each chamber
had been filled. In the meantime we'd be stuck
with fifty or a hundred arrows, or had had our
heads caved in by someone swinging a long
rifle, knocking people limb from limb. There
was no glamour in my father's work. Until
at last we shot the gun. Suddenly all the effort
expended itself at once, and then the full "report,"
the gun roaring. All his life he busied himself
with nails and nubs and slides and plates
and files and little weights and tiny distances.
He could work five weeks on a "die," then have
it break in the press, they'd tell him, for
being "slightly off." Or maybe from somebody

else's error—no matter—or file the metal off
too thin on one side, off by a millionth of one
inch, after weeks of labor, then have it break,
the whole thing wasted. I have one of those
dies on my desk, a lovely flower pattern, all
petals, a flourish of flower strangely chill in
its steel, but one crest broken off where the press
came down or where the stainless snapped
the die. I can still remember the motion he
would make when something failed, of throwing
up his arms, and rocking back, like the famous
ethnic joke where the person having the hard time
figuring out some simple thing, like screwing in
a light bulb by turning it the proper way, strikes
his forehead with the flat of his palm. If it
worked, the satisfaction of having it "work."
When the Colt fired, the satisfaction of hearing
the roar, and then the smoke surrounding us
like an applauding audience, pressing in to
touch the masters of the wizardry. After five
or six shots the smoke would lie upon us
like a pall, like night itself, and you would
wonder how at Gettysburg, for instance, anybody
knew who to shoot, how you could not see a
thing, except be hit perhaps by some stray
bullet, fired at random into the "fray." And
the nail fell out of the shoe at Gettysburg,
and the horse was hobbled, and the rider fell,
the horse stumbling, pitching the rider forwards
over the shoulders of the horse, breaking his
neck against the ground as he struck. In his
leather pouch perhaps a document, a map, or
message scribbled quick, to "move" or "hold,"
which then did not get through, the courier
dead, his leather pouch thrown forwards in the
weeds, never to be found. So upon the field

of battle, lines swayed and wavered, and the troops
that should have come sat in their tents all
afternoon, under a hot and broiling sun, played
cards, took naps under the shade of trees. My
father had strong glasses for "close work."
The smallest things magnified to gigantic
proportions, was why he threw his arms up
skyward when the drain plugged or the gun
failed to fire, its powder being wet, from sweat
in the barrel, some natural condensation from
a dewy night, who knew the long process
awaiting, the long thin rod with the hard wire
coiled at the end, to snare and grab the ball,
and yank it "free." He would talk of how
the "rifling" of the famous Kentucky rifle
was cut, the hours and literally weeks of labor,
before machines idled both horses and men.
He made work of everything. We would go
camping and the ground where the tent was
to be placed had to raked, so that no twigs or
stones might lie under its floor. So that, days
later, walking barefoot, from out of his
sleeping bag to pee in the night, he would
not stub his toe or jab his heel down hard,
piercing the skin. Or take the whole tent down
to set it up again! He was a perfectionist,
working with what he knew, doing meticulous
things to numb, unfeeling wood, or hard,
unyielding steel, coaxing some definition
from them, some form of truth. A poet of the
probable—disaster or adversity—each thing
quite possible, but with the proper effort,
and luck too, that was always part of anything,
the care that went in, over and over, getting
it right, checking and double-checking, and
I can remember the lists he made, and lists

to back up other lists, then making shorter lists,
scratching things off when done, only to find,
thirty miles out, nearly to Old Forge, he'd
left the sprinkler on out on the front piece of
lawn, or a basement light burning—pull to
the side of the road, the horse dead under him,
the battle lost...and then the War beyond!
My son says "Fuck it," then starts over with less,
each time more free, less encumbered. His
greatest metaphor is from his recent trip,
driving off with his canoe atop his car,
running out of money for gas, or the car
breaking down, instead of fixing it, selling it
there "on the spot," perhaps "for scrap," or
trading it there and then for tobacco and beer,
then setting off again, each time to reinvent
the self, throwing the canoe into some river
then, and going on, each time turning less
into more, into whatever was needed, into
sufficiency, another dawning. "Fuck it"—
that would make my father throw his hands
up in front of his face. I am of two minds, the
bridge between the less and more, bridge
across the generations—the one so crippled
by possessions, the other so free of them—
with only the soul for company, or even less,
the breath, going along keeping time by the
sound of your own heartbeat. A battle rages
between two armies, one racked by doubts,
McClellan in the early months of The War,
the story my father knew and told, how he
would overestimate Confederate strength,
and thereby would not venture forth, but sat
forever in his tent, the letters back and forth
to Lincoln, Lincoln urging him to move, then
more delays, more lists, more fabrications and

excuses. My father must have seen himself
in this general—how could he help not to?
But loved the Lees and Grants, the dashing ones,
or Sherman best, those who did not look either
ahead or back, that infamous march to the sea,
leaving the land in ruins behind, everybody's
ideal hero or barbarian. It must have been relief
to read of such men, my father when not working
his head buried in another Civil War book,
seeing there full well judgments of life and
death hung on a slurred word or a lost message.
My father always looked back, and looked ahead into
what he had not done yet in the past to ward off what
the future might behold—trapped between the
two somewhere in the limbo of the present,
afraid for what he had not done and had not yet
to do. Uneasy in the saddle he sat. The shoe
beneath one foot of his horse not being sturdy,
or perhaps too worn, the horse aged, weak from
a recent illness, or who tires easily, sweats from
even a short walk, the iron in the nail imperfect,
its shape mishammered, or brittle with impurities.
He could have gone further in his estimates, for
my father knew his metals well, surrounded in
his shop at home with blocks of brass and steel,
big chunks of lead, copper and tin, wrought
iron in different attitudes. There in the
humid cellar they would all discolor, or
pick up dirt off the floor, until you had
to open them with drills to know their depths.
I used to love to pull down into a block of brass
with a bit, working the drill press handle
another quarter of a turn, the drill bit screwing
down, the bright curl of the shaving coming up,
a wondrous curlicue. Or he would come home
from work, his shirt all littered with steel shavings,

shiny as gold or silver, bright medallion-color,
still warm from the work. Covered as if his
chest shimmered in medals of courage, ribbons
of the wealth of empires. I thought of my father
as I drew the nails out of the boards of the old
garage six years back, hand-forged, some of
them still blue and new, all shapes and lengths,
no two alike, pounded on the forge and anvil
of the blacksmith. Perhaps some imperfection
weakened one, which might have held a shoe
in place, a bit of ore not fully hot enough and
did not melt, a bit of the grit of the earth itself,
resistant to its liquid state, to lodge a weak
spot on the shaft. The pressure, growing, of the
pounding, the horse really lathered up, the run
hard, would work the metal back and forth,
until, at last, at this weakest spot the nail
might snap. Then its big head fall off in
the dust. So for the shoe then, weakening from
its weakest spot, now where the nail was gone,
the shoe slapping back and forth too much,
too much "play" in it, until its movement pulled
the other nails out, each one falling in turn,
for there is always one that's weaker yet,
working their way around the shoe, until
the last one, maybe strong and hard as Mom
herself, might fall. (Are we still waiting for that?)
My brother was the nail found wanting. Not
of good metal made, his alloy not of the proper
mixture for both flexibility and strength, heated too
slowly or too fast, too soon from the oven come,
his fibers not fused enough for that harrowing
decade of many deaths, second son and to
the shadows come, his horse lean and hungry
tethered in sparse grass, his booze or drugs
rusting his joints and armaments, take your pick

of any deadly sin—or idle time? Or the wrong
friends? Or something scribbled in a hasty
note read wrong. Whatever was that fatal
alloy? Pulling free then, the nail breaking off
or falling out, the shoe of himself coming off,
the strange composite beast a family is,
that walks or staggers on eight legs, the party
horse under the Navaho blanket, each person
pulling in his own direction, the creature mostly
blind, the whole if held together by whatever
passes for love or blood—stuck—first the one
to fall, to stumble, like a horse, each person
one of the composite legs. We had walked
strangely from the first, as many said, with
little Jeff the short leg of the beast, then,
as if to bear the full collective weight of
time and all its lies and truths, collapsing under
them, unable to bear up, and the rest falling.
So was the horse lost. And who the rider?
Some ascendant idea of family, some perfected
union of our opposites, some ideal uplifted
from the common beast-state of the lot of us,
in our communion or treaty what message?
What war that waged beyond we could not
go to now? The mad-glad armies flowing
all around us like some raging river, while
we sat there in our ruin, these wounded and
forlorn. So the world went by us when Jeff
died, and we stalled out, unable to proceed.
Who ever rides a horse on three legs?—
They are put down. And their names written
on air or water in the hallows of regrets.
A year I retraced the course of his run,
sorted the fragments of his gear, carry his
key ring with me still, with its little silver
coil and the purple bead, hand cast it seems

like. Jackie took it in her hand last night,
and looked on it, some artifact from a lost world.
She put it down again. This might have been
the very nail itself, too beautiful to do the heavy
work it once had been intended for, wrapped on
the key to the car they let him drive, all those
raging horses under its hood. His hand caressing
the coil and the bead, sparkling as they did on
the arm of his thought, forged in some other
light and life, distracting him from what he looked
at, forgetting the road ahead, maybe a gift from
some lover yet to know, to run headlong and crash
into that bright oncoming car. How does the famous
saying go? The battle lost? And then for the want
of the battle, the war? And so on, and the throne to
wobble on its three legs, the king—great So-and-So,
and everybody at each other's throats. The way
we were in 1863. The way we were in that
September. So was the ruin general and complete.
All thoughts of empire vanished. In ancient scenes,
in comic books I read, behind the glory center of
the frame, always the rest stand, sorry in dilapidation,
moving hunched over our labors, the simple cart,
the horse with a limp toiling in harnesses,
wheels wobbling, the worn iron of the shoe,
the fragile nails to clatter on the cobblestones.
Attend them well, these faces strange and known,
these little people and their little cares. His
words, my father's words, ring down through
all the years to me. Well have I learned the
terror of their poetry, both doom and prayer.

The Eaten

You see them in fields.
Along the edge of roads
standing abrupt in the wind
like blocks of salt,
or in a fenced-in yard
with blocks of salt—
an hour to kill they stand there
looking south—a day—
or turn and walk a few feet
to look through the slats of the gate,
or poke their broad heads through
barbed wire to get at a little grass.
You see them always hung up,
their whole heads and necks
jammed through the wires,
reaching, reaching,
anything to get a little change
in the routine,
the long, forbidden reach,
sticking their necks out,
not thinking what it means.
Or there is the famous scene
come upon so many times
of the loose calf
out beyond the borders of the yard,
it stands there in the road
or not so bold as that but
in the ditch
astonished it is somewhere else,
not knowing what it means,
reckless and jumpy,
eager to run, or having run,
eager to run again,

if only in its mind
there might be somewhere it
could get away to,
some promised land
beyond the long, established
sameness of the day,
the sky pink at morning,
blurring to blue, the lone sun
up and staring, watching
like a guard somebody's
posted on the hill.
They want to run away,
or back in time
before we tamed them to
this drudgery, this standing
around, waiting to die,
heads down gentle in the grass,
offering the flat of the face
for the hammer blow,
the throat to cut and
let the rush of hot blood out.
Once they were of the earth,
once they knew essential
things, the rush of water
in a stream, the feel of
water over rocks,
the chase among the wolves,
under the moon,
or standing in the dark,
alive with the night,
asleep and yet awake,
the inner eye adjusted to
the dark, the rawness
in all they did,
and run like the wind itself,
clatter of hooves over stone,

kicking the dust up,
breathing the fresh heat in,
riding the hillside down
into sweet valleys.
Gagged, they were taken
and dragged, clubbed and shackled.
Strapped and tied, and made
to bear. They walked forward,
as if to escape, but were
turned at the edges of fields,
and made another dash
gone back the other way,
bearing the plow. Their young
were taken from them and changed,
until they did not know them,
bending down, some memory
lost, light gone out of
their eyes. What wildness
in the bull remains, is kept
apart. One lone bull to be all
what they were, to keep
the strangeness of experience,
the smell of blood,
to pound the earth to dust
and charge at color.
They are made sport of,
confused, pierced, tortured,
then on someone's schedule
slain by a flick of the wrist,
the whole grand mass brought down,
a living train wreck, to
lie like garbage in the dust.
Thus is their race mocked.
Thousands neutered, left dazed,
to stand in the wind like billboards,
trying to remember what they knew,

or herding to escape the heat
down along a hollow
where a creek runs. They
stand among the trees, or
lie in the mud, one turned this
way, another that, with glazed eyes,
plagued by flies. Only their
tails move, flicking, flicking,
while the sun drops lower,
goes down further a bit. You
and I are also flesh. We walk
into the same day, smile,
grow angry. Milling about,
among our own kind, you would think
us just as tame, just as subdued,
except that one of us is doing
handstands on the lawn, two
have crossed the grass to throw
between them brightly colored
spinning orbs. Another on her
way back to class draws castles
in her head, writes of her cares
and fears. "Dear Mom. I saw
the most amazing thing," then
tears the letter up. She will not
be ruled. Not even by caring.
Slams the door leaving her room.
The mind will answer nothing
but itself. Even asleep, in a
life that does not constrain it,
it assembles, it declares itself,
and rises, all at once, in brilliant
explanation of identity:
"I was a fool today. I was
rambunctious, flippant, said
bad words, said what I had

to say. Fuck you!" And then
in a bar, on any night, a
fist flies, then they are down
and coiling in one figure.
Some raw wound that will
not heal, under the one moon.
Now, in a field, we gather
them. A thousand in a
field you look at once,
and in a blink, and never
look again. A thousand
walking where they have to
walk. Above them the holy
sky does not split, does
not send thunderbolts or
the red arm of God.
Only the sun. Food is
mashed in troughs. There
is another place where water
steeps in a hole, is warm
and sickening. They stand
in their own shit,
walk to the left where
the hot sun bakes the
earth, or to the right
where the shit piles up
a mountain high you could
climb up and take the view,
and I saw once a cow
there, on top, the
hero of the day, apart,
unnoticed, unseen, and I
saw another lot with a huge
mountain of shit heaped up,
like some holy temple—and
"To what god it is they pray?—

Please tell me."—
which they are building up
from their own entrails,
poisoning the waters and
the winds of Earth. Each breath
each takes they take in the foul
stench. They draw a breath,
and then another breath.
And so they are free to die,
at last, and glad to die,
one ride in a truck, a short
furious ride with fresh air
over them, a look at the green
world, and the ground
rushed past as if they ran
as formerly they ran
over the grass and the
hills. Two in
a truck I saw this
morning, two of the
living dead, shit-caked,
their bodies like extensions
of the filth they live in,
staggering for balance in
a wobbly truck. They
nuzzled each other, cheek to
cheek, eye to eye,
nostril to nostril, excited
and alive, happy to be
going somewhere.
What have we done?

The Yellow Tree

For John Brehm

It stands, has stood, through this
and many autumns. The yellow tree.
I see its branches of order and disorder.
It holds, as they say, the wind, through
this and what is left to come, the winter.
And I am renewed in it. I take flight when
wind through its leaves nudges them, when
from a distance I see its stalwart presence,
there beside the building in the dark
its leaves make. What is it calls me back?
What is it calls me out from my delirium to
stop my steps and put my briefcase down,
to feast in its light. And under it
its fallen hands, to curve their outreached
fingers up. What is it a symbol of? What
was there seen in the dark of the past of
my mind, imprinted here again, holy and
sacred? The yellow tree. I love the sound
of the words. "Tree" which is still with
sounds, and then the "e," the ease of the "es."
And yellow to mellow in, to soften in the
folds of those sounds, yellow for light
in a room of soft pillows. How can there
be such a pairing without delight? To
walk on towards it, to step, from out of
my car, my mind extended there on wires,
frantic and headlong, and then to move
towards it on my two legs, it standing
fast, tied to the earth. Do I wish myself
more anchored in some fact of my place?
While beating on madly my heart goes,

seeing it flash in the light, die in the
cold. Sleep comes over it the way sleep
comes over the old in us, to take us
down, rooted at last in the weight of
bones. Bonelike branches stem and
reach, stiff in their gray bark,
fleshless, like rock, while all around
the flags of the soul flash like suns.
I love this yellow that this tree
without a thought or choice cannot
but wear, its code against dismay, its
coat of all one color for the gray sky,
the brown of the brick beside it, the
green of the attendant lawn. To take
it down and wear it in a shirt, my
radiance, a fond display that says
I am of nature too, and wear it proudly,
some unthinking hue beyond discord or
the jangling of nerves. So on their
shields, out of stories, we get knights
and kings who carried them aloft, on
banners into the fray. So is this my
banner borne aloft. Index to my spirit.
Moment to moment it keeps my time.
Midnight it bears its yellow under the
white moon. Dark hour of reconstruction,
the mind looping back in dreams, to rub
my cares again, and put new faces on fear.
It endures through that. Morning the sun
caresses it, from its far remove, its
distant palace, splashes its tears on it
to sharpen all the edges of its leaves.
And all the day the wind tugs and tears,
to pull another leaf down, to harass it,
and then another day it stands more ragged
than before, more bare. While I am there

the process seems to cease. The wind
runs off, like a wild dog, leaving the
tree to me. And I can detect beneath
the thinning cover of the leaves,
the strength of permanence. Where did
I go to be gone and lost and not to know?
How did my mind race wild across the sky
like clouds, now to come home? The yellow
tree. In its enclosing touch I would
devote myself, and sink myself in its
beauty. Nowhere to know it more, or
feel more centered in the earth. No
mind more clear than when I look at it.

Money

I write out simply and without distress
the check for the diamond earrings
I am buying for my wife. I just
came drifting in off the street,
and I am in a hurry. The salesgirl
likes how sure I am of everything.
I looked a little while at rows and rows.
Some were too small, like in The Three
Bears, and some, My God, too big.
I turned them over on the back to
peek at the price. Even too much
for me, I thought, at times, though
I had the money. And some were just
right. Do you do gift wrap, I inquired,
and then wrote out my check,
unhurried, and without anxiety,
free from a moment from all my fears.
It's a beautiful thing about money,
to sit on your wallet and feel how
fat it is, or stand on the top of it,
like king of the mountain, to take
on all comers, or like the eye on the
top of the pyramid on the back of the
dollar bill—is that where it is?—
all that width across the base to
emphasize stability. And you can
stand there and survey the world.
Last year at this time I remember
I would sit in my favorite bar
and nurse a cup of coffee half
the morning and the afternoon,
paying my bills. I'd write checks
for an hour, eat away a little

at my immense balance at MasterCard,
like a little mouse in a
grain silo, eating and eating at the
bottom, until, perhaps, stuffed,
he'd move and the corn on top of
the heap would shift a grain or two,
then level off again like a gold brick.
Finished, sitting in my own sweat,
I'd have all of thirty dollars left
to last the month, paid out by check
a couple dollars at a time, coffee
and toast, and leave a small tip for
Cheryl or Kim, then package up my poems
and walk out into the snow. In writing
poems I had developed a peculiar style
of printing with a fine-point pen, two
columns to a page, starting out in a fairly
long line, maybe twelve or fourteen syllables,
then slowly narrowing, until, by the
time I reached the second page
each line was no more than seven or eight.
Or six. But maybe fifty or sixty
lines to a column, the printing so small
I could get an epic poem
squeezed onto a page-and-a-half.
When my father died and I wanted to
write a poem for his funeral, I sat
in the kitchen with my daughter Jax
and squeezed the whole thing out,
all three pages single-spaced of typing,
the man's whole life, and everything I
had to say, on a single sheet, indeed one
single side. (Things have been different
lately.) The object, I suppose, was to
save paper, not to wear out too many trees,
not to wear out too many handles of my

briefcase carting the load
back and forth. (There in that house
where a nickel could last a month,
setting on the countertop, unthreatened.)
My daughter sat with me, writing her
poems. Her sheets flew thick and
fast, like someone, maybe Liberace,
playing the piano with his high flourishes.
She'd write a word, then reconsider it,
then start another page—some rich man
somewhere pays her bills, keeps her in
paper, sandwiches and beer. There it was,
my father's whole life, meaning and
purpose, reduced to a few obituary lines
in a poem. I wanted, as they say, the
personal touch. Not to entrust his going
off, his final presence and his brand-new
absence in the room, lying there,
to strangers. And anyway, I had the
money. Who better to say what a man's
life means but his only surviving child,
trained for years at university, to sit around
all day staring at the rain, trying to find
some proper syllable, like a glass or gauge
to catch it in. Smoking cigarettes my
father paid for, that I had charged to
his account at the local bookstore,
that's when every would-be poet
had a Pall Mall dangling from her lip,
the window just behind me washed
with rain, and on the desk, also bought
at some expense, some fragile writing
instrument. We are held together by
money. I dip in my pocket, take out a
twenty, hand it to my son for two hours
at his math tutor. He's the guy down

the hall. Maybe they play cards, or
drink. It's no big deal, it isn't mine.
It's money my father left me, I the only
child, all that we did to each other, all
that we did for each other, all that
we never said to each other, and
the touching we never did, except
towards the end, my body nearly out
his door, taking his hand in mine, I
can still feel the feel of it, his hand,
soft, passive, but the skin hard from
work, from a lifetime's temper of tools,
but feeling nearly helpless nonetheless.
He had not raised that hand in anger
for many years. He had not hurt another
person in a long long time. Just a brush
of fingers, sometimes to linger, as if
the very hands would speak. Regret in
that touch. Then we were out the door.
What had those hands been doing?
Tucking money in a wallet, writing
numbers in a record book, recording
balances. Opening his closet door,
there to survey the many racks of
pants hung down, almost touching the
floor, the pickle jars resided in the
glimmer of what light could reach them
and their flash of coins. When he died
and it was certain he was dead,
when the word came from his brother
Bill, that there was all this work to do,
a household of antiques to figure out,
we went there through the snow, and,
climbing the stairs, someone, Mark, I
think, threw back the door which only all
those years my father moved. The kids

loved the coins. There were pounds of
them, tons I would want to say—but
you would laugh at me—but far too many
for some normal day. You know how change
collects unwanted in our pockets or our
purses, or in the little console of the car
I can have two dozen pennies—what good
are they? At our house Barb will scuff
my loose change off the counter by the
cellar door and pour them in a big
grape juice jar—it's our Europe money.
(We've been saving six or seven years.)
The bottom of the jar is maybe five inches
deep. We're forty years from filling it up.
Dad had his big pickle jars, the kind
you see at the market down that special
aisle where everything is oversized,
not family-sized, but for a generation or
for a whole season, the way they used
to live back in another century, the whole
cucumber patch salted down under a lid,
and stored in a cool place. These big jars
held perhaps three quarts, not quite a gallon,
the size you buy and save big money on,
only you have to make room for on a shelf,
and after a couple weeks—I mean, how many
pickles could a person eat?—the jar got shoved
back, out of the light. So my father
ate his pickles, saving money, and the pennies
that he saved by buying the large, economy
size, which lasted a year at least, he dropped
inside the pickle jar he saved as well, after
that last sour pickle was gone. Filled with
water, brine and cukes, one might lift the
jar out of the cart, and up on the conveyor belt,
and hope the salesgirl did not make a joke,

but filled with pennies, or nickels, well,
you could hardly budge them. Mark lifts
weights to keep from being bored, so we let
him wrestle the jars out into the light.
Dad must have left them there for years, and
the money bags, and only had to go there,
once in a while—how often did he go there?—
and unscrew a lid, unscrew a lid with that
soft cool distant hand I touched on my way
out his door. Then drop in the money.
Screw the lid back on. There were four or
five big pickle jars of pennies. One jar was
so old it was half full of wheat backs. Mark
said, carrying it down the stairs to the kitchen,
"Dad, it's full of wheat backs!" So we spent
the whole damn night at the kitchen table
sorting through until our hands were filthy
from the copper tarnish. Everybody saves
something. Barb saves green stamps,
and, finally, one day we got a phone,
a portable, that when the battery goes dead,
we can never find it. We can turn the whole
house upside down, then to go back to
the one on the wall, the one tied down,
the old reliable one, that's always in place,
the way my dad was. So my father went to
his jars, and opened the door and put the
light on. You might forget how many there
were, the feel of them, the weight, from
last time when you looked. I hope it
gave him lots of satisfaction. There was even
an odd-looking box with metal sides and
bottom, with, inside, fifty or sixty rolls of
pennies, where maybe he was getting them
ready for the bank. If he could part with
them at all? And I thought of the scene

in the great movie *The Thing*, the remake
of it, where underneath the warehouse, in
a tomb of ice, they find the tiny space ship
the monster's been building from scraps
and parts. How busy he's been, the hero
says, out here alone with no one to talk to.
There were bags of money. Half dollars,
a whole heavy bag. A big bag of bi-
centennial quarters, maybe five hundred,
and I thought how seldom it ever was I
saved a quarter, let alone a half dollar, which
I then carted off to the bank in Uncle Bill's
Chevy Suburban one morning through the snow.
And cashed in for bills in big sizes, so they
would all fit in my pocket. Money's
embarrassing. It's great to have, but not in
pennies. And I thought of all the people I
could put off their feed by paying what I
owed in pennies—say an expensive restaurant,
with four waiters, like we just had had,
New Year's Eve, a couple days before
my father died, to finish and wipe my lips,
carefully, one last time, then pull from
underneath my chair thirty or forty pounds
of pennies, then pour them all over the table
top. Sue gave me a bad scare when she
told me after I had taken the quarters in,
that they were worth a buck apiece, how
the girls at the bank must have thought it
was Christmas still, and I imagined when
I came back in the next day—it took me two
full days to take the money in—they'd be
all lined up waiting for me, cheering as I
came. But she was wrong. I parked right
in front, and when I opened the back door
one of the big pickle jars, as if it were

alive, like something out of *The Thing*,
from pressing all its vast weight down onto
the car cushion, bobbed a little up and
came down plummeting to shatter at my feet.
I had to pick through glass and snow, to try
to get the pennies back again, a handful
at a time, and cut myself three or four
times, and froze my fingers too. If only
you could see me now, I said aloud, to
have my father hear me. To see me here
doing your work, or worse, scratching in
the snow with my bare hand, trying to get
each last cent out of you. For how is it
a man's worth is measured? And laughed
at how foolish I must have looked. The
girls inside could not take the wet money,
their counter machine would short out
if we poured the snow in, and there was
glass as well. I had to take the whole mess
back in a rug and lay the glass and pennies
on the floor beside the furnace, and turn
them every hour, like chestnuts roasting,
or like the greasy French fries which my father
would turn over in the oven when I lived with
him, to brown the two sides, before he salted
them, and which, as I write here, realize is
what it was that killed him, too much grease
and salt, his arteries all plugged, nor all the
money in the world to make him well.
My father died of a heart attack, January 2,
1991. It does my own heart good to know
he died in a hospital, under the watchful gaze
of nurses and doctors, which only the rich
can afford nowadays. Not because I want to
blame the nurses and the doctors, but because
I want to think my father cared enough about

himself to treat himself to an overnight stay,
perhaps in their luxury suite, at whatever
outrageous price they're asking now.
He was in there, Bill said, only for a couple
hours really, dying of a massive attack,
not living long enough to deplete his vast
reserves of pennies, leaving them all to me.
It was all very "convenient." Dying, as he
did, as Charles Bukowski says in a famous
poem how his father did, saving on hospital bills.
There were hundreds of dollars in pennies,
hundreds more of nickels and quarters and dimes
and halves. And a big bag of Kennedy half dollars,
made of silver, which I was not so stupid as to
cash in, but dragged home, starting my own
hoard, to leave for the grandkids to find.
Uncle Bill said, when we walked in their door,
"Before I forget here is your father's wallet—
There's a lot of money in there." There was.
I think perhaps six hundred dollars, maybe more.
Later going through his cards I found a fifty
folded for safe keeping. He kept money secret
even from himself, perhaps for having so
few surprises in life, some sudden shock of
finding an extra fifty dollars he didn't know
he had. His whole house was like that.
Each hour, it seemed, we came upon
another treasure. Another thing unlooked
for, some hidden secret reservoir beneath
the common surface of his day. In his
checkbook, which Jax found, lying innocently
in a little desk he bought to keep his cancelled
checks in—and he kept them there—and they
were "all" there—right back to the beginning
in the garden when, being what we are, a curious
and contrary sort, we ate of the sacred tree—

he had—twenty-seven-thousand dollars. So
much that the girl whistled, I think, or sighed,
at the bank, when we took the checkbook in
to clear his account, and I sighed too, and I
was proud of him. And there was other money
too, I won't bore you with the details, nothing
risky of course, no wild defense stocks, just
good solid savings like a trickle of pennies
in a jar. It was amazing, how much "can be"
saved, even on a small retirement, and a
long lifetime of hard work, getting up
every morning at five, putting his two eggs
on to boil, then shaving in the bathroom with
the bristle brush, working up the lather in
the shaving mug. I loved my father. I do
not want his life to be over. I do not want
his money or his furniture, but see him
sitting on one of the chairs he saved from
the second-hand store, refinished, the wood
almost new again, and reupholstered, sitting
reading of his precious Civil War. Reading
about all that vast expense and waste, while
he saved pennies in a jar. Well, the next day
I went back with the pennies I'd dried on
the old carpet by the furnace. It took me
ten minutes to get them all into the cloth
bag, trying to pick the pieces of glass out,
and pieces of lint. Back at the bank, we
poured the contents in the hopper of the
strange money-eating machine that clicked
and clacked and registered the growing sum
in bright red numerals on a special gauge.
It stalled right away, choking on a piece of
lint, or a bent penny, or probably a shard
of pickle jar. Then went into its funny
humming sound, not unlike you hear

on a heart monitor, when someone's heart
stops beating, and the long line starts.
That's when I got out of there, and drove
around the block, and ran a couple errands
in my head. I was still somehow under my
father's spell. Made more perhaps for all
this adding of him up. He had died, but
he was still alive, persisting in the common
coin of the realm. A sort of universal man,
who plugged into the daily give and take
which is our lives. He seemed alive with light,
the shine of the coins themselves enveloped
me, as if a holy light. And I was safe,
I could do nothing wrong, almost like the
nursing infant close at the mother's breast,
taking its nourishment, protected from all
dangers. And—what shall I say—intimate
with my father, perhaps for the first time.
We did have one final surprise. The very
last day, closing up the house, with lots of
people over helping clean and carry stuff
out to the Ryder truck, I cleaned out
the perishables from my father's refrigerator.
There among the wilted cabbage leaves,
among the swollen pickle jars with their
fat middles so like us when our waistlines
swell and our pants split, among the cans
of no-name soda pop he bought "to save
money," and which he would never drink,
and no one else could drink, I found a
Tupperware container. Looking through
the opaque milky plastic I thought I saw
what looked like a piece of meat, maybe
an old leftover pot roast dripping grease,
which now he would not get to eat.
Inside was a purple leather bag, with its

drawstring tight and wrapped around the
top. "Watch," I said, turning to Sue,
who was helping me sort through food,
"This bag will be filled with money!"
And it was. There was quite a lot. White
business envelopes, with the money inside,
stacked, then folded, then folded again,
and a rubber band holding the whole thing
snug. There were a number of such
packets. Most filled with twenties, and I
thought of how Barb could carry a twenty
around in her wallet all week without spending
it, skipping lunch, working through the noon
inside her room, showing me the money maybe
a week later. But in others there were stacks
of fifties, then some hundreds, side by side
or head to tail like sardines in a can. It was
the sort of thing people killed for. In my Dad's
favorite Old Western movies, holding up the stage,
breaking into the strongbox, shooting it out
with your formerly best friend. In a purple
leather bag, my dead brother Jeff's bag,
purple my brother's favorite color, cut from the
leather we bought with him once to make
that pair of pants he did not live to finish.
It paid a whole lot of our bills. It paid for
our plane tickets home, to come back for
the funeral, and for the Ryder truck to haul
his furniture back. It paid for our kids' tuition,
whose money we had put aside, but had had
to spend on the plane fare. With it I also
bought two new orange-shafted Bic fine-point
four-color pens, the ones Ray Ronci thinks are
funny, to write new poems with. And
today, walking into Wards, I bought some
diamond earrings for my love.

The Patience of Job

Was I his horse he put a saddle on
and tried to break? A colt, frisky and
jumpy, always somehow in trouble?—
the world suddenly dropping away
at my feet, the way the sand fell out
from under me at Old Forge that hot day,
when I went in, over my head, and had
to be pulled out—I can still see the dark
shape of the fish turning away, or was
that some dark angel come to fetch me
for my sins?—and then my father leaping
in behind, his arms outstretched to bring me
back to shore, to sputter on the beach, gagging,
then to resume—was it minutes later?—
or years?—daring to presume again?
Daring to breathe and go, run and leap
into some other heap of mischief.
Or fall on the floor, in fever, the world
aswim before my eyes, heat devils swirling
in the hall, as under me he slipped the
stretcher of his arms—then rubbed me
down with alcohol. For going out beyond
my depth it was—for getting myself too
close to the flames—where everything
about the world was strange, and dangerous.
Then would I sit sullen, sulking in my
stupefaction, already askew in some
new direction, maybe a splinter in my finger—
when Presto there he was, aswim before me,
new eye fitted into his old eye, focused down along
a beam of light, a long sharp needle probing
in the shallows of my pain. In the shop I was
treacherous, always smashing my thumb—

good thing that I had only two—or leaning
on the workbench watching him fix something
I had broken, rubbed my upper bare arm against
the bench light, bare bulb burning all the night
in its hot socket—he pouring the butter
on—I can still feel it, smell it, the home
remedies he knew which probably his mother
taught him—and might have rubbed me down
with Scotch whiskey instead of rubbing alcohol,
till my skin came off in his hands, the very skin—
and the skin on my arm curled up and peeled,
where he rubbed the butter on. At the lathe,
where I insisted I work, he gave me
a cutting tool to use, and a piece of stock
locked in the chuck, spinning, making a blur,
and I would press in with the tool, curling the
wood off in some ecstatic spiral, up over my
shoulder, till there was nothing left of it,
reduced to nothing but a stub. Then its revenge,
the night it ripped my thumbnail off, just
lifted it clean, out of its neat compartment, the
skin so smooth underneath I thought the nail
still there, until I touched it, nearly fainting. I
saw him bend, out of the corner of one eye,
under the table saw, retrieve the nail—
where it went probably in some collection
that he kept, parts of my body I had lost,
that he might reassemble me again some day
when I was down to nothing, just a nub
left standing. The spectacular wreck of my
bike, just two weeks new, down that alley
steep past lilacs on both sides, fragrance,
sunlight on my face, not stopping at the corner,
remember him cradling the bike in his arms,
after he'd cradled me, the front forks bent,
the front wheel all askew, wobbly like

some cartoon wheel. Patient he took me home.
Patient he fixed the bike. Patient he gave
it back. Impatient, reckless, a wild hair
up my ass, I hastened off again to my next
disaster. My favorite story was the story
of the toad, of Toad Hall, the Magnificent
Mr. Toad, always rushing here and there,
going faster, going quickly, never looking,
always outstripped by something better going
faster past him toward disaster—until he had
to have it too—"Whoopee!" Toad cried—
the terror of the countryside, high over hill
and dale—I can still see his eyes bulging out,
goggles blown back crooked on his eyes,
wind making a flag of his scarf—
and then the fatal crash: into the donkey cart,
into the milk wagon, the milk cans spilling
off in all directions. Toad in a sling, Toad
on a stretcher being borne away, only
to come back some other day. He was always
picking himself up, as I was, and setting out
bravely again, always with an eye on novelty,
and soft for innovation—you could put a rocket
on a scooter, Toad would buy it, tearing
off into the sunset of the—Yikes!—headlights
of oncoming cars. Then home again for his
rehabilitations, Father "waiting on him hand
and foot," getting me stood up again, ready
for the next onslaught. Whatever I'd break
he'd fix. Though it might sit two weeks, or an
interminable two days, two hours or two
minutes, while my heart stalled and leaped
all over the place, sputtered and failed, swooned
and crashed into the deepest darkest gloom.
I was an instant fatalist. If, with one pull,
the mower might not start, then it was gone

and done, the day ruined. Seeing my bike
in pieces I was doomed—never to ride the wind
again, or fly with the birds—fly like lightning
off to Vogel Park, there to descend in tiers
down branches of the Christmas pines, great
limbs that dipped me down, then swung me back
up skyward—how far out could I go on a limb
before it bent down nearly to the earth
then lobbed me up into the afternoon, then
crashing harder for the heights I dared ascend
to. I was all pits of doom and flights of ecstasy,
wild promise taken on the crest of the tide,
then backward downward thrown onto the rocks,
into the very teeth of night. Then buoyant bobbing
up again, back into sight, wearing my bright orange
jacket that chafed under the arms or caught my
sunburn just exactly right to make me know
I had one—then would he rub on me the healing
balm. Perhaps he could remember his own
endless flight out upwards towards the stars,
and then, ballistic, that downward arc through
shadows ever deepening, into the earth's great
gravity again. To find me, out of himself come,
toddling on my first adventure, stagger like a
drunk amidst treacherous sticks, wobbling like
a wounded pheasant up from its hiding place, or
a badly thrown football, then to come tumbling
down. Whatever I did he was there, through
rain down slickened streets, through hail and sleet,
through winter's glassy sheen on everything,
the old Chevy spinning its wheels, side-slipping
down Schuyler Street, or mornings in the snow
gone bravely off into the storm—by nightfall
home again and safely lodged. Then might
he take out his fix-it kit and stitch the cut,
or glue the wing back I had broken off, or

put the hand guard back on the hard-rock maple
fencing sword that broke Paul Ruby's rapier of pine.
The arrowhead he could not fix. Paul egged me
on to drop it over the hard concrete, to glisten
in my hand, shiny and sharp, perfectly made, a
sort of work of art but deadly too—only Paul knew
how brittle they were—I took the dare and dropped it,
then waited for my father to come home and heal it.
And took me the day Paul's backswing on his
golf club caught my mouth, killing the front teeth,
cutting the lip, and held my arm when the doctor
stitched me up—I still have that knot in the corner
of my mouth where the flesh bunched. After a
while it was clear I needed herding, or corralling,
whatever the word. Or guarding, or shackling,
or with him riding shotgun, plopped down beside
me with every now and then reaching out
his hand to do the steering, holding the reins
light but firm while I applied the whip to my
own back, jumping again and again onward to
attack or out of my own skin. In Uncle Remus,
another mythic tale, I got quite stuck in the
tarry story of the great tar baby, sagging on a
log, the rabbit, cantankerous, impulsive,
feisty, never "letting well enough alone." And
had to lay his fists upon it—for its pride of silence
in the face of—what were they?—his taunts and
insults. To get gummed up good, as Br'er Bear
might put it, to "get him gummed up good, Br'er
Fox," he'd venture, swinging his log of a club.
Only to outwit them both and get "clean out of
there," back to the deadly briar patch, healed and
made stronger from his escape. I could not have
been what I was without him, could not have been
young without his patience. Once established
we sustained these roles. Years later, when either

might have wished it different, he was still
picking up where I was messing up. Came one
night through howling blizzards to get my MG started
in a snowdrift in Syracuse. Or, when I lost the
marble pool ball of the shifter handle—someone
stole it from the car outside a bar—fashioned a
new one out of brass and walnut, locking it on
with a special washer nut, so it could not be
removed. By the time I was eight or nine
he knew what to expect, would come home
cautiously, into the house—I'd see him out
the corner of one eye, setting his lunch pail down,
tiptoeing in around the fridge, or slipping
past the rack of overshoes, removing his own,
to come on soft socks down the cellar stairs,
trying to "get a little breathing room" before
I ran to greet him with my latest news.
I threw a football through the sunporch window—
it broke all to pieces, bent the blinds,
the putty flew out in big chunks all across
the room. A couple plants knocked over. I
set fire to the dry grass in the outfield of the
old baseball park, the fireman were called,
while I went running all around to try to fetch
a pail of water, stood in some stranger's
kitchen trying to talk, while sirens ruptured
at the edge of consciousness. Would take
his precious files and pound them into rocks
to knock the dizzy fossils out onto the floor,
small clams locked in sockets in the dirty
floor of some ocean I had found a piece of the
the bottom of, bending the file tips over, or snap
the handles of his delicate hammers, break the
fragile coping saw blades, trying to cut through
some huge tree I'd dragged in through the
basement window, to see the circled years

inside, concealed. I painted my boat, and
all around my boat, in some vast blue moat
that ran the width and length of the table,
for it to sail on, burned with the burning kit
right through the plastic envelopes he brought
for me to put my coins in, burning the wood block
underneath that was part of the piece of furniture
he was making, left on the wood bench next to
the drill press. Drilled down into the steel
block, pulling the bit so fast I snapped it off,
then couldn't get the chuck to twist it out,
or left the chuck in once, then turned the press
on to see the chuck fly through the window
into the back yard. My kite got stuck high in
the maple tree, where he climbed up, not trusting
me, my ball got jammed in the crotch of limbs,
then threw my bat up after it, which also stuck,
and then the rake off the garage wall.
Would cast my fishing lure to some remote
and all-alluring spot, far off across the stream,
beyond my reach, beyond my depth to walk,
where it would catch up on a log or rock,
then call him—"Dad!"—and pull the rod tip up.
To watch him struggling in the current, one
arm holding the line, the other out for balance
like a tightrope walker, tipsy against the flow,
sliding his feet along, then into the dark green
water go, and over the tops of his boots! Then
to bring the prize lure back, whereupon I'd
cast it back again into the overhung limbs
off the other bank, watching it arc around
and around, knotting itself quite good, as old
Br'er Bear might deem it. "Dad, I'm stuck."
Then might he turn to look at me, his torturer.
Before he set about again to make it right.
He climbs, in my imagination, up the straight

sheer face of a cliff, a precipice up which
I've gone, or slid down from the top of,
dangling from an outflung arm of a sickly
tree, roots gnarled on the shale of the rock
face, pulling out, my grip slipping, arms
burning, tears in my eyes. Or wedged in some
crevasse, where, turning to watch some apparition
in the snow, slipped on my skis, to plummet
headlong, catching just above the void, one
bootlace tearing free, the one ski gone, the
other caught by the toe, dangling and swaying
like Br'er Bear caught in the goober patch.
And see him, my father, just in the corner of
one eye, paying the long rope out he's carried
all this way, just for this purpose formed, the
frayed ends scorched, the knots all tight, pounding
the long steel shank of the stake into the blue
throat of the ice, then coming down hand over
hand, losing his aviator's hat, to grab me firm around
the waist and lift me clear. And save me for another
year. Father, tireless one, endless upon earth
you went, redeemer of my vast embezzlements,
as against Nature even and God I went, traducer
of you always in my trespasses, snarled in the web
of my own making, spidered, lame, transfixed in
the gum of my own confusion, loose did I go
reckless upon earth and time, healer you came through
thick and thin, uncomplaining, as I was unrepentant,
may you rest easy now, as I, myself a father, dutiful,
take up your tasks, lay out the bounty of your
temperance, adjust your smiling mask.

The Stars

Back from "The Marsh," still wet
from where I walked in it, I
clambered down the steep sandbank
above the rapids and the pool.
It was almost dark. I could hear
the roar of the water, and maybe I
could see the crests of the white
waves as the water boiled down
over the rocks. I would cast
for that. I had cast all day,
so I tried to remember what it
felt like, what the distance felt
like, throwing the lure. I did
not want to cast too far upstream
where the rocks were. I put on
my black lure, the one with the
black feathers over the hooks.
Black was good on the river before,
at the big falls down in the canyon,
forty miles to the East, and two
years back. We caught some great
trout with it. So I flipped
the lure, into the noise of
the falls, and the dark. I
felt it land, felt the line stop
sliding through the guides of
the pole. I cranked in. Faster
at first, to get the lure moving,
to keep it off the rocks and weeds.
It came. I felt it nudge the rocks,
felt it catch a bit in the weeds
that grew there, the long strands
of cress with the circles of

soft, lacy leaves. I reeled it in.
The angle of the line increased
as the lure came on across the
pool below me. It came nearer,
and the rod tip was almost over
the place where it was in the
stream below. Then I reeled it
further until I heard the metal hit
the end of the rod tip. Then I
brought the rod tip back, depressed
the button on the reel, and cast again.
Three times I did this, holding my
breath. Five times. Nothing.
Nothing but the rocket ride of
the falls, bumping the rocks,
snaring a weed or two. Three times
I had to reach my arm out
and pull off a cluster of weeds
attached to the hooks. Then,
free once more, I cast again.
I thought to try another lure, a
flatfish I bought at Cabela's
famous store in Sidney. I reached
into my vest, and took out the
lure box. Felt around in the
box for the lure. It was big and
puffed up, hollow, I expect.
There was some light still left
in the sky. I removed the old lure.
Then I held the flatfish up against
the sky, inserting the end of the
line through the loop of wire on
the top of the lure. I thought I
had it but I missed. I tried again.
I could not see the thin gray line
against the pale gray sky. The

sky had all the light there was,
but it was the wrong color. I
needed light behind me, or in
my eyes. I needed my father's
miner's lamp fastened on the belt
around my head, to see what I
was doing. Three times I tried
to thread the line, then gave it up.
The little wire loop of the flatfish
flopped around on its pivot point.
I did not have enough hands
to hold everything, the lure, also
the rod, and then to thread the
line through. I gave it up.
Mark came down the bank. He
asked me for some snelled hooks
he might use to put trout
liver on for bait, to fish the
pool below the falls. I had
cleaned my two little trout
in the water at my feet, but
saved the heads and the entrails.
Mark had his flashlight, and poked
around in the guts. He found
the liver. Pushed it onto the
hook, then doubled it back,
to push another lobe on.
Then he walked off left along
the bank, to stand directly above
the pool. He let the bait fall.
He placed the light on the shore,
so that it shone out onto the
water. He could see where
the line went down into the
pool. He waited. I watched
him wait. I waited with him.

I lit a cigar. The air was chill.
I liked to see the red glow off
the tip of the cigar. I puffed on
it until the ash formed, then
brushed off the ash. The glow
was revealed. It seemed a lovely
light. No fish. Nothing was
hitting. I put the old black lure
on and cast again into the sound.
Again it came down hard over
the rocks, bumping and snagging.
Then pulled free and came on.
I tried another cast. Maybe I
threw a little harder this time?
The lure stopped. I could not
reel it in. I pulled on the rod.
I pulled some more. Trying to
free the lure. I pulled again
and then the line snapped.
It all came back at me, limp
and dead. So I was done with
fishing for the day. I had made
perhaps 500 casts. My arm
was tired. The place I stuck
the butt end of the rod against
my gut was sore. I climbed
up the bank. Mark and I went
back to camp. There was the
bloom of the tent, darker against
the grass around it. Damon had
turned the car lights on. Inside
the tent Craig had the stove
going. He was frying potatoes
for dinner. He had the stove on
the cooler, using it for a table.
Four trout lay on the cooler top,

waiting to go in the pan. I
handed him my other two, from
upsteam where I'd caught them
earlier. It felt good bringing home
the food. Then Craig put the
trout in the pan. They smelled
good cooking. Then we all
came into the tent and sat around
on the floor. We had two forks.
We ate in shifts. First Jeremy
wrestled with his fish. He did
not like it much. Craig gave me
mine. It was delicious. I pulled
the long bone out of the soft
flesh, splashed on the tartar sauce.
I was hungry from walking by
the stream, from fishing all day.
I sat on my legs on the floor.
It felt good to be dry and warm
after having been wet all day.
Mark ate his fish, finished what
Jeremy had left. We cleaned up
the mess. When we got outside
the stars were out. I had never
seen so many. Everywhere I looked
there was a star. Stars and then
beside them other stars. Brighter
ones in front, but then if you
looked past them you would see
another. Right to the edge of
the hills. No light pollution here
as in the city. In the city
you could not see the stars along
the edge of the sky. I was surprised
to see such bright imposing stars
all along the line of hills. The

sky was full. From East to West,
from North to South, everywhere I
looked. I turned around, to face
another way, and there they were.
You could even see The Milky Way.
"That's The Milky Way," I said,
"I think?" No one could say.
We did not even know our own
galaxy, turned on its edge in the
sky, the great wheel we ride.
Too long we had been in the city,
inside our houses, watching TV,
or bent under our lamps reading.
Here was the sky itself, in all
its radiance.

Getting Ready for the Auction

I go from room to room
in my father's house, the day before
the auction, getting ready to take Claire
Hill to the train station, and make my
rounds among the tables of objects,
taking photos, trying to hold onto
things still even as I let them go,
as John Brehm says my poems are about,
trying to save things from Time, and
I reach out my hand to pick something
up, and hold it for a little while,
a second or two, waiting for its energy
to fill me, for images to enter my mind,
and, if nothing there, if nothing comes,
to put it down again and pass along
to the next object, knowing there will
not be time to hold them all. I put
my hand upon the cover of a book,
Sinking of the Titanic, which Barb
wants to save, consoling ourselves that
our disaster, no matter how far it might
have taken us, into strange waters, or
dark seas of our imagining, is nothing
compared to theirs; the Currier & Ives
calendars Aunt Helen sent, and which were
saved, like everything my father touched,
writing his own poem, each day another
image, another line or two; the Audubon
prints, which Claire looked at, looking
perhaps for a match for her living room,
but then put back; the large display map of
Oneida County, charting our place in the
world; the red yo-yo, with rhinestones,

four on a side, one rhinestone missing on
one side, and didn't have the time to turn
it over, the paint chipped from "Walking the
Dog" or some other maneuver I never
mastered. I worked it, or whatever you call
it, and it ran away across the carpet; a small
green clock, stuck forever on 12:15, reminding
me of World War II, with two short brass feet
so it can lean back on its rim while you
fumble in the dark near midnight, forty years.
The Wonder of Trains, bent from being
wedged down in a box, nor any time to study
its pictures; a strange, inlaid tray, oval with a
concave diamond inlay in the middle, marked
by a band of fleurs-de-lis or pheasant feet in snow
around the rim; a washed-out oil painting in a
fine pine frame, of a woman in a bonnet and
long dress, pausing as if on the road of life, or
garden path, flowers to her left and right, the
path like a stream bed, basic color green, two
people behind her, the woman taking the gentleman's
arm, he wearing a tri-cornered hat, and which they
tell me was my father's favorite picture; a Ringling
Brothers and Barnum & Bailey whistling billboard for
my own American Flyer train set, vintage 1950,
and which I can hear still rounding some bend
of track beneath our Christmas tree, calling in
welcome or some long farewell; my RFA black
onyx class ring, 1962 (Oh where were you?)
which Les Porter our auctioneer found, and
handed it to me, standing in the living room,
and tried it on, finding it did not fit, the house
quiet around me, all the junk around me, this
day a day I never saw no matter how it was
I stared into the future, and Barb and Claire gone
shopping for my birthday—I will be forty-seven

tomorrow, the day we bury my father's junk,
or pass it on as in some weird relay race,
passing it all to others now to carry on into
tomorrow; a box of Paganini violin rosin, but
no violin, the rosin wrapped in cellophane held
in a cork frame; my Colber Corporation metal and
tin bridge, Irvington, New Jersey, for the train set;
three plastic put-together cars, one with the driver
still in place, bent over, already old, the large smear
of his mustache being prominent, remembering how,
gluing the halves together, the halves which didn't
line up, as most things never did if you looked close,
and the pale thin paint which barely covered the
bunched, rippled top of the roadster; simulated cone
trees with caked-stuck paint for snow; the metal
toy cash register with keys mangled, perhaps from
my trying to make it pay; the Simplex Practical
Typewriter Number 300, which somehow printed
from a large rotating disc, but I cannot make it
work except it gives its happy clicking sound so
like my Smith-Corona on which I am now typing
this; the bell which my mother just now saw today
in the copper tray, with which either Jeff or I would
summon help if we were sick with measles or the
chicken pox, one ring for measles, two for chicken pox;
the large meat tenderizing mallet, with tenderizing face
on one side, pyramid-pointed teeth; the chrome cheese
grater, like the plastic one from Grisante's here in Lincoln;
my brother's guitar-string tighteners, also chrome, and
over in the corner a cheap guitar in some stage of being
refinished, soon to be gone; the green canvas cot with
aluminum tubing for a frame, very uncomfortable as I
remember, from weeks of trying to sleep on them up
in the mountains—and what were our dreams then?
The cookie jar in the shape of an apple, painted yellow
for some reason, but with its two large lobes of leaves;

and I enter another room, another decade maybe to
find one Rival electric can opener, with its outlet
inconveniently behind the wall space, thirty inches wide,
between the wall and knotty pine sink frame and cupboards
Dad built, in a happier time, his project taking months,
or years, I forget, to stand among other projects, now
unfinished, and which I will not finish; assorted wooden
kitchen tools, looking like back scratchers or obscure
sexual devices; a 1940 activity contest motorcycle racer
Trophy, from Jeff's room, who raced only on roads; the
book *How to Build and Race Hotrods* by Griffith Borgerson,
from ARCO, part of their "do-it-yourself" series; and the
do-it-yourself tin lid from our camping water pail,
with a wooden knob crowned by a pewter flower, a
zinnia, I think, round in shape but with two flats opposite
each other to slide in under the handles of the pail; *The
First Book of Bugs*, with *Bugs* in huge orange-red
letters on the cover, and the letters with cilia and spines
as if made from old saguaro cactuses; my Grandma Estelle
Bradshaw's treadle-style 1903 Singer sewing machine,
beautifully decorated with gold vines and red, football-shaped
objects, lined out in gold paint, too heavy to fit on our jet-ski
trailer for the trip back; the Boston Rocker, a reproduction,
which no one enjoys sitting in, it being either too tall or too
short; the souvenir Francis A. Sullivan Democratic candidate
for city judge six-inch ruler—"Your vote will be appreciated";
Indian corn cluster to greet guests no more, off the
back door, where going out with an armload of boards
I sliced through the screen—no matter—and pushed on
to a box of one dozen Blackfeet Indian Pens, from Blackfeet
Industrial Park, Browning, Montana, 79 cents; a stack of
cardinal hotplates, wings uplifted as if he just touched down
on something hot; two ashtrays fluted in the shape of large
hand-shaped leaves; a yellow tulip, stylized, wood, on a small
round base and wooden stem, blooming strangely in the
perverse garden of the tabletop, while over in the corner the

Green Air Force sub-40-degrees-below-zero sleeping bag,
taken from Griffiss Air Force Base, which was too hot for
these our temperate climes, and lay stretched out in the hot
attic for thirty years; my first tennis racquet, painted black
by me in one of its endless transformations; the gun rack
on the tabletop with on one side the yellow spindle pine lamp
rising up out of a white hobnail base, no shade, while on
the other side the old trap thrower hanging on its leather
from a gun notch; my first and only microscope still in
its original wooden crate, where the first time I looked
at a slide I rammed the big 300X Tasco lens down onto
the wool-fibers slide, busting the slide plate cover, which
then developed all these lovely fracture lines, which I
then, of course, confused with the fibers, sheers and splits
of canyons and crystals; what's left of our happy yellow
dishes with their apple tree; a small red book of telephones
and addresses, empty; a box of shoulder patches, military,
and brass buttons which father bought, probably at auction,
and which now I give back to war, and one lovely pin
of an airplane propeller, silver, I think, and later stolen
during the auction preview; ram horns mounted on a
board, with their marrow like old desiccated cottage cheese
staying behind as the outer horn material tries to slip off,
curling as it comes; my father's personally designed two-
room cottage tent, made for him by Milvo Awning and
Tent Works, Rome, New York—I found the bill of sale
among my father's papers, $135, and which we would drag
back and forth to and from the North Country in the rain,
our Dad's vacation, and string up in the attic or garage
like desperados from the rafters; the screen popcorn popper,
for a campfire, which we never used but father never tired
of hauling back and forth; the book in paperback, *East of
Eden*—my Dad took me to the movie of which I remember
two scenes, the rotting lettuces, and then the old man,
the father, with his stroke—No, three!—James Dean in
the ice house sending the blocks down—and did my

father think it was good for me so young to see here
such a wild, rebellious boy?—and almost forty-seven now,
still mad at the world, only now mellowing out, having
had my most recent fight with Mike Donohue over my
Dad's old truck, heart that will never rest, heart that will
never be still; old *Playboys*, with, in one, a photo of
Floyd Little and the other All-Americans, Floyd who lived
on my floor my junior year in college, the dorm name
I cannot remember except that it was twenty stories;
compass I never learned to use, vowing now at forty-six
to steer clear of uncharted wastes; bongo drums, which I
bought to play in a band, but one night all the other boys
on their guitars, and I who could not keep the beat,
or make my hands fly fast enough; my Viewmaster with
my favorite Sam Sawyer disc, and its best scene of all,
the fight with the octopus, Sam being rescued by the
swordfish at the last, sticking its long snout into the
monster; one record on the Playtime label, two songs
by Jimmy Blaine, "Arkansas Traveler" and "Turkey in
The Straw" on the flip side—I can still remember those
tunes, and the sound of the needle in the heavy metal tone
arm digging deep into the groove as I sat beside it, so
close my arm nearly touched its arm and made the needle
jump—which pictured two bearded guys, one in the
rain with an umbrella, looking Amish in a stiff black
hat, the other in a striped shirt holding a violin like a
big wrench under the stars; my Easter basket, the bigger
one, I being the first son, and Jeff's, the smaller one,
both made the same but why did I get so much more
than Jeff?—and more years?—Jeff dead at twenty-five,
I nearing fifty, and still my basket twice as large as his;
banners from the Adirondacks, made of felt, printed with
Indian heads and headdresses, a souvenir of Raquette Lake,
another with a long canoe—which I "collected," though
I don't recall I ever had them on my walls, some from
places I had never been, Whiteface Mountain and Lake

Champlain—even then it was far better to imagine life
than live it, and I could dream of those places, and say
the words to myself—Lake Champlain—with my eyes
closed; hip boots and waders, recent light-weight efforts,
but one old heavy rubber pair I wore, feeling the chill of
the water rise up my leg, and how in deep holes in Fish
Creek it would rush in over the boot tops; my father's
private reading stand, his last attempt to build something
entirely from scratch, but which never worked, the book
board flimsy, made of paneling—where was the thick and
solid wood of yesteryear?—the frame made of plastic plumbing
tubes and elbows, three platform feet, which somehow would
never sit flat on any floor, but the brackets that hold the
platform on the legs of heavy burnished steel and aluminum—
such an obvious failure—and which I could not decide to take
home after the funeral, not wishing to remember him for this
final foolishness, he who had built so much so well so long,
and cannot decide now, standing in the cellar of his decimated
shop, to keep or not to keep?—I compromise, taking the
finely wrought brackets and the board, leaving the almost
obscene base of curved white entrails—from which I would
build some day my own reading stand, not stick in the basement
out of sight—how much of all this vast array ended up treated
like this?—too good to throw away, for the man who never
parted with anything, who lived as I said in just one-thousandth
of his stuff—or in his own words, "just scratching the surface,"
sitting late at night with the light on in the sun porch under
a brass-plated reading lamp, while Bill slept—like the brain of
a dinosaur, high atop its long neck over the huge body, a tiny
light of a mind; and the old snowmobile he was hand-crafting
from plywood—I found the skis on a shelf, which he had
abandoned as he had abandoned his marriage after Mom left,
who, in the words of his one true friend Bill Pasternak—sweeping
his hand around—"Who in the end was not comforted by this!"—
sweeping it across the whole array…a man who "deserved better";
then here on the table beside me the two-man saw we used to

cut the burl off the yellow birch, and I who nearly wore him out,
pushing where I should have pulled, coasting as he pulled,
to bind the saw again and again in the cut—how exasperated
he must have been to have such a fool for a son!—who had,
as mother said, "the patience of Job"; and then the burl itself,
that he was going to turn on the lathe to make into a lovely
salad bowl with its grain all tortured like the ribbons of the
brain, or like the brain of my brother, who, when I told Bill
Pasternak of my grief at my brother's death, said "No, Jeff
was lost in his own torment"—as out of such torment
beauty may sometimes come; the miracle pancake griddle,
another failure, this time an early one—why do I dwell so
much on his failures?—or why did he keep them around—
perhaps to ensure his humility?—but were there really
so many triumphs that he needed by these to be humbled?—
with the top sheet stainless, where the pancakes would fry—
and the bottom sheet of brass—to take and hold the heat,
whereupon it being placed on the stove, curled up
like a leaf, the two metals having such different
"coefficients of expansion," a lesson you might read
about in physics class, but never take to heart...one of
Les Porter's men, Smoky maybe or Scott, I saw with it
a couple days ago, carrying it out to the sale tables,
which as a joke on the world I figured I will let them sell—
to pass the lesson on of how imperfect we are; the lid
for the white enamel pail he called "the thunder mug,"
a memorable elocution—his language was colorful—
which we took camping, how in the dark of the mountain
tent Mom would get up to pee, tossing the toilet paper
in, and which was then my job in the morning—how in
the bright sunshine with the heat high I would have to
carry it through the woods praying no one would see me
on the trail, always taking the remotest one, then to make
a mad dash through the final clearing, fearing to drop the
lid down the hole, our urines mixed more closely than our
bloods; my brother's gray chest for his leather-working

supplies and his silverwork, which Mark ransacked looking
for silver, containing still three big Bowie-style blades,
roughed out, and with the file work or grinder work done,
and a wooden mock-up throwing knife, a unique design,
which maybe Jeff was going to try to build, and which I
kept; and the next-door neighbor's son, Augie Pasqualetti's
son, who has throat cancer, shocking me yesterday carving
a wooden Bowie knife for his beautiful son, exactly like
the ones Dad used to make; Dad's chrome single-mantled
white-gas lantern, which he prided himself in, because it
threw more light than the big Coleman twin-mantle, though
in order to achieve its brightness made a dreadful racket from
its high pressure—you had to pump it maybe thirty times to
get it cranked up—so that to sit by it at night you could not
talk or listen to the wilderness, which Dad being deaf did not
seem to mind—how everything bears its own consequence and
has its own logic, and we look at something at auction and so
little of its reasoning comes through to us—how Mike last
night, another man of tools, stood in the near-empty cellar
and hung his head, but stooped to take a single file from under
a leg of the bench, and touching it named it—was it a "half-moon"—
it wasn't a "rat-tailed"—I know a rat-tailed when I see one!—
who could stand for hours in my father's shop and untangle
the mystery I saw everywhere I looked, touching and naming,
as I could not see, or see in the face of my father his illness—
could look at him and did not see his death; and I am in the
sun porch cellar now with the old bottles I dug up and
gave to him, which are worthless but which he faithfully
kept; and how I sold his old fishing reels to a hungry
guy who could not look at me, in a cloud of dust, was
how I knew I had made him a good deal; my brother's
underwater spear gun—I have that famous photo of Jeff,
upstairs in the hall just outside the bathroom, fat in his
bathing suit, wearing his beautiful rubber-handled stainless
knife, with the saw teeth, swim fins, mask and snorkel,
and who would soon turn and go into the room on one of

his deepest dives; the fencing swords with the taped handles—
Dad sawed the points off, which Mark and I hit together
today, I explaining how we just made noise, though Mark
parried me and pulled my sword out of my hand, he having
the stronger wrists; the bicycle-wheel boat-carrier Dad
built, to take us up the trail to remote Cheney Pond, one
of our great outdoor adventures with Bill Pasternak,
who, when we could not handle the weight of the boat
and the outboard too, picked up the 7-and-a-half horse
Evinrude and put it on his shoulder, which I was reminded
of when Bill stopped by to see the fix we were in.
Barb calls to me from upstairs. I am standing over Dad's
folding reflector oven, the one we used to set up in front
of the campground fireplace and bake potatoes in. Made
of shiny stainless steel, with little slots for the shelves to
fit into, and Dad made pins to hold it all together, it
still looks brand-new. It is time to go to the train station,
so I say goodbye to the oven and my brother's inflatable
rubber orange canoe in its blue bag in the corner. We
drive to the station, park across the street. Out in front
are steel benches which look just like the little benches
I had for my train set. There are people sitting there,
just as there were when I was young. I carry Claire's
suitcase in through the big doors of the station.
Unbeknownst to me, she is taking one of the little
benches with its tiny creased people home with her to
Erie. Of all the things we had, and offered her, she liked
these best. They will come to occupy a section of her
shadowbox, along with her thimbles and knick-knacks.
The next day is the auction. Les Porter will be his usual
eloquent self, praising my father for having brought
together all these splendid things. And they will all be
sold, dispersed again throughout the world, as light is
dispersed in the sky, fading as we say goodbye. Claire
boards her train, taking her treasures with her as the day ends.

For Kay Patterson

It shall not be wasted, your breath,
the slant of your shoulder, the way
your nose upturned, or your eye looked
aside. We will absorb the way your
voice came to emerge, found in itself
a confidence and depth, and then
came out, to fade again, and let another
talk. In Nancy that voice which is yours
is shared, resides, and will be kept, as
pieces of your thought comprise our minds.
We are built up out of the earth.
Father to daughter, mother to son,
sister to brother, each and all,
the measure of ourselves, taken
from lost things fading. In a field
we walk as if forlorn, in the dust
of ruined civilizations, to come
upon a fragment which we keep,
to notch and use to hold our keys,
the way my father touched my arm,
which is the way his touching is
preserved in mine. We live with
the dead, and through them. We
come forth in the places where once
they stood, and which they abandoned,
we come to stand and make those
places ours. Your clothes will
be worn. Your way to the diner
after work, though it is lost in all
the million ways a city finds, loses
in its disarray, will be walked.
Someone will eat your lunch, sit
where you sat, watch in the sky the

cloud that might have seemed to
you a shape. In your brother Rodney
is the mouth from which you made
the words which marked the poetry
by which you lived. Strange is his
mouth now, kissed by yours, yet
will he find its proper shape
and turn. He sits beside us. He
reaches out the reach of his mind,
extended that much further by your
sympathies. What was once yours
is his, to add to in the store of all we
need to keep in order to withstand
your loss. Living, you learned the
way, and went, to teach us part of
what we know of going and will
find. Dying, you made it ours.

The Place Where the Pheasant Clawed Me

is healing now. Here, let me show you.
Here, here, here, and here, and then again, over
here. It happened so fast. I shot and
ran hard up the corn row, not knowing
where it was. It was there—curled
around itself, cocked, coiled, then
uncocked, then standing up to run, its
eye aflame, and the great red eyepatch,
like a warrior in armor, the very
spirit of the corn itself. I fell
upon him then with my full self,
both hands upon him, as he kicked
and flopped. Dropping my gun in the
snow, my hat blown off in the
tussle. How long it took I cannot
say. There was no time, just heart-
beats, wingbeats, and the sun pouring
down, sand in an hour glass. We
wrestled at the very heart of the
field, far from my car, far from
my life, rolling in the snow,
and once he got away, but I lunged
out and grabbed the edge of one
wing, as he fled, and brought him
back. He had the strength of ten,
which seemed in turn to grow,
and the feet thrashing, and the
spurs raking me. One got me
here in the web of my hand,
where forefinger joins with my
thumb, and where I hold the pen

when writing, poetry of an afternoon,
sonnets to forgotten beauty,
poems to the dead. Our two
hearts beating. It was ordained
somewhere that I should win.
I outweighed my friend fifty to
one, though lacked his wildness,
and told my hunting buddies later
it had been an even match, when
I fist-fought the rooster pheasant
in Slama's cornfield. All around
us the corn stood like an audience
brought to its feet, in a huge
stadium and theatre, where the
action transpires in the midst
of the seats, and rose as I strode
with my trusty gun through the
drifts by the road, and entered
the palatial estate of the corn,
there to enact our drama. To my
left Ken walked, off twenty rows
or so, and to my right I saw Craig's
head bob as he went—Rick was too
far away, either to help or to know—
or who could be told as it happened?—
no one—not even the pheasant as I
caressed him with loving hands—
or holding him off at arm's length,
to keep his spurs from my eyes,
on this, the last day of the season.
And I thought of that, of those
that would die on the last day,
why it should be, and would have
taken myself away to hide myself
in the shame of whatever hunger,
or walk with my animal self

between rows of corn, as if in
some primal landscape of desire.
And put my feet down in the places
marked for me, as if in endless
rehearsal we had done this,
over and over, a million pheasants
and a million men, joined in a
blaze of sunlight amidst snow,
wrestling on the ground they
are barely uprisen from, I so
briefly upon my own two feet,
then to fall upon him in the
snow, like my animal self
being given something that it
understood. Through the rows
I walked, westward, tramping
down the snow, and kept my animal
short on his leash, or chain,
when the pheasant appeared,
leapt as out of one of many
prisons of skins. Called by the
wild. And fierce appearance of
my friend, dressed in full
battle array, blazoned with
every kind of color, prism of
the sun, bejeweled in light's
blood—dark rose of the splendor
of what is. They are so beautiful,
these creatures, killing them
you break down into tears, for
how unlovely you are, or I felt
that I was killing myself, or
some pure angel of my sight,
for how much I admire what they
are, and can almost not do it,
cleaning them, stripping off

their body glove of skin, handfuls
of feathers, each feather a painting
intricately filled—and once I
spent a whole afternoon
taking them out one after another,
each in turn more lovely than
the one before, asking what
had I made my life long
upon earth that is one tenth so
beautiful. We are not worthy
of them, these extravagant jesters
of the corn, barbaric birds of
the wind's fire. So as I lay
in my embrace of him, I knelt
on the earth to beg forgiveness
for this fierce life. In my hands
I felt him die. First the wings
flapping less, so like a heartbeat,
so like my own in my own chest,
then the beak cracking open,
and the eye gone blank. To lift
him at the last as a shudder went
through him, feeling it go, outward,
like the soul's taking flight—
like pheasants from the ends of
corn rows—a sudden palpitation
of the feet, or heartbeats, then
to stumble upwards as the wings
catch—then they are free.
In the truck I sat there
bathed in sweat, or sipped my
lifeblood coffee—it was cold.
In the back he rode, like so much
garbage to the dump, the wind
kept ruffling him, and almost
rolled him over as a wing grabbed

at the breeze—did it call him
still? Beside him two more
angels lay in rough disorder of limbs,
lay where the dogs lay down
tired from their labors—and
brought him home this Sunday
as the sun set on the last day.
Look at my hands where his
spurs cut. See these scars to mark
me still when he is gone back
to dust. Here, a notch cut in my
knuckle, and then this scratch
along the heel of my hand, and
here, most deeply, in the web of
my hand, where the pen fits,
to hurt me as I tell his story.

Weeds

for Echo Easton

I saw the weeds today,
and thought of all the rank disorder
of the world. I was just leaving
Crete, and had my window down,
and looked to turn left on some
side street, and they were there,
a whole apron of them out to
the curb, vibrant purple flowers
on short stalks, mixed amidst
twisted foliage. I'm not an
expert, I did not know their names,
but remembered my own wars
down through the ages. Our
victory is rather recent, in fact,
maybe four years ago we finished
off the last of them. Oh I still
have wild onions out back near
where we had the asparagus,
and which are spreading East
and West across the slope.
From my window in the kitchen
I can read the onslaught—
frantically dialing the phone
to Seward, to bring the spray man
out—why won't he answer my call?
But the rest are gone. Bindweed—
was that what it was?—you could
scrape your fingers over the
ground like the tines of a rake,
and all the little networks of vines
would break off—and load an armful
up, but which would all come back

again. Or I could spray the hell
out of them—chickweed, lamb's
quarters—I didn't know what they
were—and stare at the photos
on the can—the dreaded dandelion
given a primary spot in the gallery—
precious yellow of childhood's
green romp of a dream—to come
home with my knees stained
from lawns I fell on dead a hundred
times—arrows and bullets in my
heart. To make a vase of dandelions
for her—who stuck them in a water
glass and lodged them on the
windowsill. Beneath the streaming
sun come in to kiss her cheek over
the pork chop pan. Against childhood's
incessant yes I dragged out hoses
and the little globe of death—the
spray jar with its milky orange fluid—
and went around like a spaceman
on his leash—childhood not yet
banished—and loved the secret
surge in the nozzle when I stuck
my finger over the vent hole.
That's when the poison siphoned
up—to lay the healing killing spray
upon their broad uplifted hands.
We had some truly terrible weeds.
A purple one with a small showy
flower, the leaf quite pretty with a
filigree—I never looked too close—
drawn to its beauty but repelled—
its smell was horrible—is the world
grotesque? Or lovely? Both.
Somewhere at one end of the

spectrum we might place the orchid—
beauty so rare and fragile it seems
impossible—breathe of it in
passing and it's gone—like that
girl's face in the hall—a moment's
recognition, a sudden bolt of energy,
like lightning without light,
then the crowd closed, milling.
Down at the other end the
weeds in Greg Kuzma's yard—
famous for miles around—whatever
errant pod blew in from outer space
or Mars, took root in our fecund loam.
There was one horrendous one
I'll never get over—even just
a few of them amidst the grass
and the mower would blow
a fetid cloud, to send chills
up my back! I'd have to stop
the mower or stop breathing, and
push on through—though sometimes
it would clog from the stems,
and choke to a halt like me. Maybe
it could not stand the vile odor?
Then, nearly sick, sweating, I'd
have to stoop down to their level
to unsnarl the blade, my hands wet
from their blood. What gave them
life?—the sun itself to shine down
lordly on all things. If given a chance—
say my neglect of two weeks in spring,
not mowing, they would rise up,
towering above the grass. To bend
beside a clump of them and pull
them out around the flower bed, then
try to shrug my hands off—what is their

infamous name?! And go to rub
my hands under the faucet or smear them
over the dew-laden lawn. I was
unclean. Even my skin seemed wrong,
shudders up along my arms, my
back all goose bumps in revulsion.
Upon close inspection—if one could
make it—one might detect small purple
flowers in a V beneath the leaves,
the stems tortured a little, not
unlovely to look at, and once I saw
a bee there, a big bumblebee, the
kind of bomber science tells us
cannot fly, and yet it does—bumbling
against the noxious blooms—and
I wanted to yell to save it—or
imagined its honey—put up in
coke bottle glass five inches thick,
and stare into the purple ink of
those depths, disclosing what?—
the worm in the rose, the skull
beneath the face, blank eye pits
turning with maggots. What
morning of shame and bitterness
to serve that honey over the
breakfast toast—to retch that
sick concoction all the way to
work, or stagger off into a field
writhing. And remembered my years
of the bitter life—harsh harvest I made
over my brother's grave—mowing
those fierce flowers of unrepressed
anguish. After his death the
yard was my punishment—
and get the old mowers out, strap
on my sweatbands and go, a warrior

to my sacrifice. Everything
rank and vile spoke of his crushed
head Ken Boyd worked so long
at, so at the last we could look
upon my brother, built-up putty
over the brow—and found his
finger bones beneath the walnut
tree. Barb asked at last, the house
intact finally after all her efforts,
why we could not have a real
lawn like the world—while I
condemned to penance expected
no less, and made excuses.
We had too much shade, I told
her, or grass could not be made
to grow on land so hilled, no
order tame the vastness of this
wilderness—clutching my pain
to my chest, puking the vile
breath of the weeds. So was
my father before me martyr to
labor—to failure—and before
him his father. Magician of
the crippled hand, slower than
the eye could see, abracadabra
over the empty hat of the hill,
to bear the rabbits stillborn in
the hat, or chomp them up in
the mower, running the nest over,
fur blown out in all directions—
small cries amidst the splintering
and the roar. Beauty was savage
then, the beauty of punishment,
beauty of justice blind—a bandage
over the eyes, one hand holding
the nose, so as not to retch. It would
take me eight hours to mow in those

days. A terrible ordeal, when, far
from the house, the mower stalled
out on a dog bone—and sometimes
think I'd never get home again,
but push the grimy mower into
the garage, and fall down weeping.
Two-hundred dollars of chemicals,
three-hundred pounds of seed,
we built a lawn. Barb started it off
one winter—over the dirt where
the weeds had died back, she
walked like some goddess, and lay
seed left and right over the
misguided earth. Spring's warm
swells and sweet rains later
the grass came full in a symphonic
bliss, then to enroll the hunched
back of my labor—until, years
later, Dennis Isernhagen jogging by
one evening, while I am outside
on my tractor—I saw his eyes flit
up the hill, taking the whole scene
in, all our palatial estate, vibrant
and thick in chemical green.
So was the wilderness tamed,
from shore to shining sea,
tangles made smooth, the vermin
snuffed out, and in Nebraska,
all around me for a hundred miles,
the land put to the plow, disked
to ordered rows of profits.
But the worm in the rose is not
forgotten. Once infected the wound
holds, implicit its own corruption,
or life becomes merely another
dream, to edge toward nightmare

any day at all. Much as I wanted
to be respectable, and rise upon
my two legs counted in the public
hall, and make my civic cry,
such things might come too
late in this our wretched century,
Auschwitz as final metaphor—
and were the Jews our weeds?
It was the weeds I loved, my
brother the unruly weed in mother's
careful garden. I remember her
on the phone those long years,
exasperated to despair, Jeff this,
Jeff that, he would not listen—
you could talk to him "like a
Dutch uncle"—what difference
would it make?—and had to be
smashed in full fury of speed and
iron—now in a manicured cemetery,
registered neatly among the rows,
complies to some profound,
irrefutable order. And Mom who says
that she's at last at peace—knowing
finally "where he's at." And I got
well, in time. One day I woke healed,
all my scars in place, to stride
forth into the chaos of mixed intents,
all beauty as my province now.
So the weeds rose up today
beside the street, upon a narrow
wedge of lawn, in the midst of
life, before a dwelling deliciously
shabby. I saluted them, wholly
as they are, holy from God come,
to comfort my unruly mind—such
beauty—and I remarked their
color in the sun.

And Then I Saw the Man Who Had No Feet

for my college roommate Serge Jelenevsky

You could have less.
This is what this "magical saying" of his said.
You could be alone, perhaps, walking
home from school, no cookies at the other
end. Or sitting in my class, embarrassed
by my 93, while Paul my rival
had a 98, then turn around and
see poor Ronnie with his 64. But I get
ahead of my story. The full enchantment
went this way—and say it out from
memory after forty years—"I was ashamed
to have no shoes, and then I saw the man
who had no feet." He must have said this
fifty times, at least, or once, on some
unforgotten afternoon, when everything converged—
sound, wind, light, rain, figures moving as under
their burdens, as in a Brueghel, perhaps the
parable of the blind leading the blind, the
group of seeming happy ones, out walking,
then upon a closer look, their dead eyes.
It was like king of the mountain, perhaps, in
winter, to sit atop its paltry snow heap crown
up at the Plaza parking lot, not much of a view,
then to feel Paul's rough hands pulling at my
coat, to tumble me down in disgrace, dirty
snow in my mouth. Or leaving my house,
then a few streets over, to go to Ronnie Arico's,
all the furniture confused, the windows in the
wrong places, a door that would not close,

some inverted universe, and watch him eat
raw eggs for lunch—what?—was there no
water to boil them? No pan to fry? And had to
fight to stay there, where I did not want to be—
the boxing gloves hung from the nail in
the cellar, and lace them on, and punch my way
back home. I still feel the scuff
on my cheek, the leather burn across my chin.
It was worse elsewhere. Even his shirts seemed
wrong, his name, and when they called on him
no answer came, as when they called on me,
without thinking I knew the story, the spelling,
the sum, the quotient. You could be less—
you could be someone else. Like Jim Ezell,
sweaty and fat, who walked beside me
on the way back from school. How did he get
that way? Wedged and swollen in his clothes,
suffering the heat, and it even a cool day—we
walked along together side by side, into the
future, into different futures. Jim Ezell, where
are you? Write me if you see this poem.
The method seems to be "consolidation." I
was up at the top of my class, my friends were
other kids who worried about grades, loved
words, talked a lot, each time around, each
change, we got more refined, like spinning
in some centrifuge, the rarer metal sifted out,
the rest discarded. But in the beginning
it was all quite raw, nobody knew, nobody
even knew your name, your name did not
mean anything, and sat beside each other in
first grade, boisterous and crude, even the
girls were not defined, and Gillian Jenkins
(now dead I learned this summer back in Rome)
beside me, huge but caring, and Mrs. Hawkes
who strode among us like the tamer in a cage,

amidst our bellowing. Short, but with a hawk's
eye, could see to the very depths of our guilt,
to sort us out one from the other, like sorting
strange sea creatures up from the depths,
the strangest body types, Tommy's bloated
arm, and Peggy's knees, knobby and ridiculous,
her last name Shank, to make us think about her
legs even more, but which we did not want to see,
and Dave Brown's freckles, each a little spot
of what his name said—had they named him that
because he had them? By what perverse logic
was the world made? Some accident of alphabet
that sat me down next to the smelly one, who
smelled like sweat and garlic, or the fragrant one,
whose perfume called you in, and then the
horrid blotches on her arms and knees. It was
all a mad scramble to escape the unfamiliar,
thrown in amongst others, like snakes
curling and uncoiling on each other's backs,
or puppies stumbling on each other's ears,
to struggle for the breast, but not one clear
reflection of the self, each different somehow,
yet the same, each one a contradiction of the
next, all manner and shape and size, unruly life
expressed in chaos of particulars, long noses, flat,
rolled, pushed, squat noses, sharp, the lips thick,
thin, or non-existent, hair brown or black or blond
or red or…the teeth small, bunched, thick, white,
short or long, the eye teeth pointed, the eye teeth
missing, braces in the mouth, like military gear,
a broken tooth, a purple one, one short one and
one long, or teeth with white flecks on them,
white but with whiter flecks—drawn to them
as to a mirror drawn, and yet repelled, drawn
to your own face in the mirror, yet repelled
to see it, as the others crowded in beside you

and around—as at some circus side show—
rolling their shoulders in to push you out.
And no advice for this. Nothing to ease
your passage in the world, nothing to ease
you home, come back from the menagerie,
your life among the animals, or hung down in
the vines, to swing on them, the monkeys in
the monkey house, all the mad jabber. We'd
come unto the table every night, fresh from
the terror of plurality, these endless variations
on an obscure theme, where I might have benefitted
from a helping hand or phrase, just silence—or the
food itself to magnify the madness of the world,
the purple beets with dirt taste of the ground,
carrots with sunspots, mashed potato lumps,
and gravy running down and over everything to
blend it all together if it might. Salad we kept in
a wooden bowl, hence to sustain the onion smell,
every variation on the theme of green, tomatoes
chopped or wedged, and onions, red cabbage, green
peppers—they taught me a democracy of taste,
and put me in the salad bowl at school and tossed
the lot of us—even now I don't know what to make
of it—and feel myself go giddy, try to get my balance,
lean on the rail to get steady, which way was up?—
and which way out? – to try to find some breathing
room. Big feet stepped on my feet, the row on row
of black galoshes in the coat room, trying to find
my own, each one a strange perversion of the next,
then getting the wrong ones out and trying to
squeeze my shoes in them, getting stuck, the coats
all colors and shapes, faded or washed too much, or
crisp and new, odd cuts of every sort of fabric—
would I wear that?—finding my own, drawn to it
by the smells of home, my mother's laundry soap,
not knowing what it was. Quick from that melee come—

to set oneself apart, or gravitate to others of your kind.
Then, surrounded by like minds, each year to find
myself with Paul, up at the top of the paper stack,
his grade a 99 and mine a 98, pulling away from
the crowd—people you could not talk to, did not
try to talk to, the strangeness of the world denied,
the same route taken every day to school, my same
routine, my play pants on when I got home, familiar
bike, familiar trees to climb, the old familiar reading
book, the math problems locked in their grids,
the answer sheet, on which I got it right.
Until I went no more upon strange streets,
or allowed myself to be threatened by difference—
I had banished them, they were invisible, I kept
turning away. On such a schedule the self grows
bloated, ingrown, the mind too sure of what
it is. Teachers seemed designed to make me learn.
They taught me how to speak it and I taught them
back. I learned and fast, and so they gave me more,
stood back and watched me work—with pride—
to see how much I could do, applauding all the time,
stars on my papers, silver stars or gold, or numbers
crowded near 100, skimming to the top like cream,
stars like the sky, the highest altitudes, where we
look up, aspiring, spirits rising. Any person might
have flourished in this system, but I became a
monster of success, an arrogance, swollen on my
certainties, good luck, the teachers' sweet indulgences.
From the very start I was diligent, would get all
As on that side of the card where they talked about
my attitude. I had "good study habits," was "proud
of my work"—I was my work, my work was my self,
they were indistinguishable one from the other.
A 98 would make me blush with shame, and
some mad demon makes me write each day to
get it right, even now, the mess I've made,

eating and sleeping, the chaos of the world pressed
in. Even now I'm trying for that perfect paper,
that 106 percent, and beat Paul Ruby at that game
we share. Paul Ruby, where are you? My father
noticed "my progress" and was not amused.
Became, for me, some sort of antidote, correction
for my soul—if I possessed one?—robot learner that
I was, robot learner that forgot the world, and sought to
bring me back to earth again from my indecent soaring.
He liked, I guess, bringing me down, all his metaphors
anchored in the common dirt under our feet, his horses
always with abundant and bountiful quantities of manure,
real horses with real appetites, to give me real shoulders
put to the task of shoveling their shit for them.
Otherwise I would have been a wraith, a disembodied
thing, but he would put my legs back under me, if
only then to knock them out from under me, reminding
me that I had legs and hands at the ends of my arms,
and arms below the turning of my head. Forced breath
back into my throat, and the air breathed, and miles
he set ahead of me to walk, and leaves to rake, the
lawn to mow, where, at the ends of my arms, I pushed
the mower, rolled over the baby bird, chopping it up.
Where in the palace of my sweet symphonic ear of my
bedazzlement its tiny cry came through to hurt me.
Or if he could not give me back the body I'd disowned,
well he would be my body for me, he would be the
body I denied, sweat run down his balding forehead
into his mouth, then lick with his lips. My lips they
were. We had the same nose. His teeth unlike mine,
all yellow and brown, neglected or dead, a sneer like
paint across them, a smear of emotion, which I could
not look at, nor could I keep my eyes from once I
saw it. He would stand before me like my reflection
in the mirror, but without perfection, and stood in
my way so that I had to pass through him to re-enter

the world. He made me look at him full on. All
our confrontations were standing, face to face,
looking straight at each other, faces but inches apart.
He would even echo my words, say them back to me
to let me hear them in another mouth, to let me have
a chance to hear how foolish they were, his big
shoulders turning, his strong forearms from the
ironwork, lifting the heavy plates of steel, cutting
the dies, sawing the heavy boards. While I shrunk
down in front of him, my body all but useless,
my arms gone over into atrophy, no baseball
of mine ever struck toward the stars, just the cramped
pinch of the pen figuring the problems out, the
squint across my brow squeezing my thoughts.
And bear down on the words, feeling like an absence
the weight of the things left out of them, he with
the originals, while I was but a clerk to the real world.
We could not have been more different, more separate,
yet joined by bits and pieces of a common language
(which here I celebrate), bridging now and then across,
toe to toe, spitting in each other's faces from the
fury of the frenzy each one felt. Days we would not
speak, not trusting ourselves to speak, or pass each
other warily, or he would seem so busy in his life,
the same as me, I with my books, he with his tools,
then meet perhaps in the hall, as if ordained, to
spar again, words like swordplay, words like clubs
and sticks, beating each other around the head and
hands. Survival was in it, for both of us, and shame,
to see the other in each one's reflection, standing
staring at each other, not believing this is what
we were. From him I came, and I was of him,
inescapably, as I find now, he leaning over the
keys as I write this, and feel his warm breath on
my neck—he has been eating soup—his favorite,
vegetable—the flavor of the stock still on his breath.

We became the other, strangers from each other
enough to see the strangeness there. No comfort
in likeness was enough for us. Or even come to
hate what we were in the other, unable to see it
in ourselves, but there, at arm's length, staring
back, blurting our words out, punishing each other
and the words, you could hate what you were,
and hate the other for showing it to you.
Even now I feed off him to occupy his place, take
over his mind, usurp his energies, stand in his
shoes. I had a tendency, as I have still, to pity
myself. No matter what I had to pity the
insufficiency. When things would not go well,
or perfectly—they always went well—but maybe
not so well as I intended—I might groan and sigh,
for something that I did not have, then he would
tell the parable. How many times I heard it in
my day—I was a real complainer in my day—I
was a real spoiled brat. Then he would tell me
of the man who had no feet. Could I conceive of it?
To look down at the dirty shoes I stood in, or
the sneakers with the big hole in the toe, my
big toe hanging out, maybe the one with the toenail
split I was ashamed of. To bring me crashing
down to earth again, my two feet driven in the dirt.
There where I might have towered over him, down
to his size again, back on his level. He was right,
as usual. Try as I might I could not escape. How
into numbers I had gone to escape words, how into
words I had gone to escape flesh, only to wake up
again, a bad taste in my mouth, the animal inside come
out to scratch its sour territory on my tongue. And
went to college on my genius grades, almost pure
mind I was, dragging my useless body after me,
almost vestigial. I was assigned a room in Del Plaine
Hall, at Syracuse. One of the new dorms. It looked

modern, even futuristic, with its bright panels of
something not quite green and not quite blue, some
color from another world. And built on stilts, as if
to rise up over the dirt, nor bother with such things.
And on a hill, above the town, above the town's
petty concerns. A proper setting for my lofty attitude.
He drove me there from Rome, and we went up
in the elevator, then followed the numbers down
the corridor. The room was airy, bright, and overlooked
a splendid, otherworldly park. I stowed my stuff,
whatever it was my mother thought I needed.
From far away I heard a sound emerge from out
of all the chaos of the world, to clarify itself as it
came on, and grew, which I could not identify—
mechanical it seemed, but then some interval
which seemed more human than machine,
and grew quite loud, came toward us down the
hall. We stood in the room, unspeaking, some
truce between us for a little while, while I
checked out the premises and listened to the
sound. It stopped outside my door, where it
had been quite loud not seconds before,
then started up again and came on through.
It was a boy, like me, well, not a boy, a man,
more man than boy, whose pain had changed
him from a boy into the man he was, who had
no feet, but he had shoes and legs which did
not work. And we had heard the sound of
crutches down the hall. As if my father had
created him, from out of the pure genius of his vision,
this self to save me from the selfish me.
Here were my father's words made flesh,
my arrogance to be redeemed, the strange made
whole, made well in the person of my friend to be,
the strange and the familiar joined as roommates
for a precious year. Serge Jelenevsky, where

are you! So are our truths borne out upon us
as we bring our words and wounds up, up out of common
grief, in the world's good time. So are the imperfect
saved, to lean upon each other, as we must, shame and
sorrow lifted into song.

Rounding the Horn

"Are we going to have to go 'around the Horn' on this one too, Greg?"—My Father asks me

Here now is the open sea, the
heave of the waves, the creaking masts,
and where I stand beside him
straining at the ropes, the whole
ship climbs towards the sun, then
falls, as out from under us our
stomachs fall away, we want to
fall down on our knees or lower,
to lie along the slick decks,
grabbing at a peg. How fiercely
the winds pour here, the rocks
come out so far we have to make
a huge, wide turn, almost out of sight
of land in the spray. Did he say
what it would be like, out here,
where no one puts his foot down
firm, but we are always sliding
back and forth, gaining and losing,
hanging on, one to another, clinging
to each other's shirts—the picture
I get of him picking me up by my
lapels, or the scruff of my neck,
shaking me dry, then letting me down—
so we would never have to look
hard in each other's eye—horizon
slipping all the while, the water
rising up in a great green wall,
and we the only two aboard—all
the others gone, jumped over the side
in terror, or swimming—is it?—

towards the haven of the distant shore?
They would not ride with us—rounding
The Horn! Had no stomach for our
feud—see how it lifts even The Sea—
above us, and to smash its fists
down upon our flimsy craft—
even The Sea's aroused! In port
these long weeks, nothing doing, no one
coming or going, the ships tied like
tired obedient horses to the rails—
get ransacked, dusted, mopped and
scrubbed—a month of chores, and
laying in of stores, big loads of fruit
being brought aboard, I in my sweatband
'cross the brow, he with his shirtsleeves
up, setting in a big load of "storms," to
take them down from their rack and
wash them as the sun floods through.
Men with parrots on their shoulders
sing a happy tune, the parrots echoing,
and one with a black spot for an eye,
and a gold tooth, and ivory handle of
the dirk at his waist, so hearty and
so full of fun, to traipse the level
decks of our dull work, but have
no head for seaward and beyond.
They would see us off at the pier,
throwing the long lines back, by
which we had been secured, some canvas
coming down into the first breath of
the breeze, catching a little, moving
us out. Something had spurred him—
what was it?—my reticence?—the
smirk that crossed my face like gull
shadow?—or a flinch, running a splinter
in beneath the nail, or some request

of mine, impossible again—and it
perhaps the third time I asked.
And so we would Round the Horn,
scarf thrown up tight across my
skull, knife in my teeth for cutting
free, at last, if I could not go
all the way with him, his bald head
splashed by the spray, one big wave
coming down upon him where he stood—
a shoulder over him, a boulder of
blue-gray rolling in. Neither was
captain here, neither was mate,
but both beyond the reach of any help,
must keep the other safe if either
was to live—both needed in the
enterprise—both inescapable
against the greater effort of The Sea.
Oh the storms in me would wake
and then I'd shake the very boards
beneath my feet, or run the stairs
both up and down, or slam the doors
both in and out, to shake the very
timbers of the place—then would he
lead me out and set me on The Sea—
to see what worthy craft I'd be—
and come along to watch the terror
in my eyes, and when sufficient,
when I had almost fully bled my storms
out from my insides, let my tempests
tear at the masts of my days and
nights, drunk on the roll and turn
of the tides and waves, drag me homebound
once again, dragging himself as well,
victim and victor both, or interchangeable,
as the waves worked back and forth,
both giving and taking back, in that

endless tug of war between our souls.
Over treacherous shoals we'd make
our way, letting the wind rip, letting
the ship roll, letting the sail unstrip,
then pulling it in again, to zig-zag over
and of a thousand rocks, and turn
the whole thing up on its narrow side
to slip over a shallow spot, where
the wind whitened the green,
and I could hear the scream of the
wind, or was it the scream of the boat
daring to take the wind, or was it
the scream from out of my very throat?
And so we would Round the Horn!
In any sort of weather, day or night,
go out with the lamps on the bowsprits,
almost blown out in the inky blow
of the wind just out of harbor, any
provocation, any declaration, and we
would go, to feel the deck beneath
me move, which had been solid ground,
the very gray linoleum that he and
Mom put down, all that long hot summer
week, new to the house, feeling the
kitchen slant, and grab the big
refrigerator as it went, too, or wanted
to, held by its cord alone, stuck
in the socket, wedging it back with
playing cards, and then the house
roll back the other way, the stove
unhinged from the wall, and all the
mice aswarm beneath our feet,
and my lost toy come out and slide
off in the corner, father's shaving mug
fly from its shelf, and we were
on our way. And the night my bike

went over the side, secured by a rope
he threw just as it passed,
catching a spoke, or the dog went
flapping down, big-eared, in the
surf, pawing the sloppy earth.
We'd gather later, back in port,
drenched and shivering, maybe my
shirt torn off, or his, or wearing what
the other one had worn, changing places
in the storm, wishing I had not been
born, Rounding the Horn. Once
embarked upon, or twice, the weight
of The Sea hung in me, like junk
jammed into my closet high against
the door, from months of my neglect,
which I would then not dare to
open, for all that I had left undone,
or not properly stowed, so that in
the waves it would roll to crush me
when I opened it. He taught me how
not to open it, the door to The Sea,
where the ship lay poised on the edge
of the tide, and anything we might
have said the rocks on which our
rounding might be foundered. Once
or twice we went Around the Horn,
and I remember it as vivid as the
day he died, those splendid days we
lived, how we had gone together on
that wondrous ride.

ABOUT THE POET

Greg Kuzma is Professor Emeritus at The University of Nebraska in Lincoln, where he taught poetry writing to undergraduates for forty-two years. His new book of critical writing is *Robert Frost*. He divides his time between Crete, Nebraska, and The Chautauqua Institution, and continues to edit The Best Cellar Press, and to write plays and screenplays. Kuzma continues to live in Crete, Nebraska, with his wife, Barb.

CPSIA information can be obtained at www.ICGtesting.com
Printed in the USA
LVOW06s0710011115

460592LV00002B/188/P

9 781935 218364